SUC[obscured] BUSINESS SPEAKING

A PRACTICAL GUIDE FOR THE STUDENT AND PROFESSIONAL

David A. Thomas
University of Richmond

Maridell Fryar
Coordinator of Fine Arts and Speech
Midland (Texas) Independent School District

NTC *NATIONAL TEXTBOOK COMPANY • Lincolnwood, Illinois U.S.A.*

1987 Printing

4255 West Touhy Avenue
Lincolnwood (Chicago), Illinois 60646-1975 U.S.A.

Manufactured in the United States of America.

6 7 8 9 0 ML 9 8 7 6 5 4 3

Contents

I Communication in the Business Environment

Characteristics of the Business World

The business or professional environment has some unique characteristics. These provide certain constraints or frameworks for speaking and listening which may only partially exist in other environments. Accordingly, the characteristics of the people who are interested in successful business communication are also unique. This creates a demand for the acquisition of communication skills in that environment. It is appropriate to look at some of those elements as a preliminary to this book.

Competitive

Regardless of its nature, any enterprise in which people are involved for the purpose of earning a living is a competitive enterprise. This means that someone else (or several someone elses) is competing with you for clients, customers, or audience. As a consequence, in business, there is no room for mediocrity. The question in business is not so much whether you are *doing* something. The question is, are you doing it better than anyone else?

And the competitive nature of business is not reserved for the relationships between enterprises. Dr. Florence Seaman and Anne Lorimer, authors of the book *Winning at Work,* point out that business success calls for both competition for individual advancement and teamwork for organizational advancement.[3] Failure to understand this basic characteristic of the business world can create communication situations which are doomed to fail.

Consider the young lady of outstanding creative talent who is on the staff of an advertising agency. Although she has excellent ideas, she cannot understand why the others in her department are promoted, and she is not. Although she blames this disappointment on the fact that she is a woman, the truth is that she fails to win advancement because she fails to project to her superiors just how good she is at her job. She suggests ideas, but she never defends them. She constantly gives in to others, even though their ideas are not as good as hers. She simply does not react competitively.

Complexity

Rarely in today's society is a business or profession simple. Even if the particular enterprise is small, it usually has enough size or interrelatedness with other like enterprises to create a chain of command, resulting in a certain loss of directness in the group. Communicative interaction between people is complex. The likelihood that you will come into communicative contact with varying types of people increases the importance of having communication skills.

Because of the complexity of the business world, network features such as chains of command, status expectations, and role perceptions exist. If you fail to understand these elements of the complex world of business, you may inadvertantly violate the existing communication guidelines.

You must carefully consider questions that relate to the proper channels of communication. What kinds of communication can be offered in face-to-face settings and what kinds need to be couched in written memorandums? What sorts of strategies should be employed with subordinates and which ones with superiors? What kinds of changes and innovations should be suggested and how can they be best represented? All of these considerations affect your degree of success in the communication of the business world.

Practical

In the business or professional setting, rarely do you communicate as an "academic exercise." Communication in the business setting is real; it is practical. It often determines hiring, sales, or promotions. Being a less than successful communicator in business usually means being less than successful in business. For this reason, more and more businesses try to hire good communicators to train their employees in basic communication skills.

Group Oriented

Much of the interaction in the business setting occurs within group structures, either formal or informal. Thus, in the business environment, skills related to your ability to lead and participate in groups become vital. Obstructive behavior and/or inability to function effectively within a group becomes, in a business setting, a serious obstacle to success, not just a social ineptness.

This particular characteristic must be carefully balanced against the competitive nature of business. A company must make money, and everyone is part of that group goal. It is necessary to maintain a network of associations with a variety of people. Although it is not necessary that one like all of his or her coworkers, it is necessary that lines of constructive communication be kept open. A rising young executive was dismayed to receive a poor mark on his evaluation from his superior. When he questioned the reason, he was told that he was "destructive in staff meetings." He had allowed his response to the competitive nature of the business world obstruct the need for teamwork in group decision making.

Varied

The skills of oral communication upon which one has to draw in the business setting are infinitely varied. There are certainly many conditions under which you will speak with ample preparation time and after careful consideration. However, there will be other times when the outcome of the communication is equally vital, and the conditions will be immediate. Consequently, preparation for speaking in the business sector calls for you to acquire skills upon which you can call at any time.

So, the very nature of the business world creates the challenge to those who would communicate effectively within it. The special characteristics of that environment lead to another factor in the demand for the acquisition of business communication skills. The professional person has some unique responsibilities to that business or industry. Business situations are, in essence, professional proving grounds, and within that structure, the business itself demands certain responsibilities of its employees, no matter at what level they operate. After all, we are talking about the skills and abilities that can be learned through training, not merely innate or inherent traits. Thus, it is useful to study and practice with the aid of books and educational programs such as this one.

Responsibilities of Employees

It is popular today to regard the typical business situation between employee and employer as a "them and us" kind of relationship. Yet, the wise employee or employer will realize that the fortunes of the individual are inextricably bound up in the fortunes of the organization. A slovenly, uncommunicative waitress may contribute to the loss of customers with the ultimate effect of losing a place of employment for herself. An abrupt, insensitive legal receptionist could effectively drive enough clients away so that the lawyer could no longer afford her services. In short, regardless of other factors involved, it is to the employee's benefit to develop and build communication skills that will enhance the success of the business with which he or she is associated.

There are three kinds of communication responsibilities which face employees as well as management. The responsible employee serves as an interpreter for the company, as a humanizer or personalizer, and as a promoter. In each of these roles, there is a particular sort of communcative stance that must be assumed.

Interpreter

It is conceivable that most businesses could still communicate impersonally to the public through ad campaigns with regard to their services, their goods, and their acquisition. However, this message would be totally in print, in highly symbolic form. Although such communication is important, it is incomplete. A good example is the camera business. You can buy cameras from mail order firms at substantial discounts. Yet many customers prefer to trade at a camera store, where a clerk can explain the equipment. Even in simple transactions, we like someone to talk with us. Consider your actions when you are dining out. How frequently do you find yourself consulting the menu, and then also questioning the waitress in order to interpret the symbolic representation of the restaurant's offerings on the menu? Think of the times you have asked a waitress to describe an entree in order to clarify some euphemistic phrase like "M'Lady's Fruit Delight." More importantly, consider the difference it makes when the waitress not only has the information you need but also conveys an enthusiasm for the article. In other business settings, consider the saleslady who clearly deciphers the code of sizes; the credit department employee who speaks with assurance concerning time payments; the nurse who reports clearly and fully on the doctor's instructions and translates them into layman's terms. Each of these employees fulfills the responsibility to interpret the organization to the clientele who need or want its services.

Humanizer

In this day of huge corporations and highly impersonalized technocracy, all employees at every level have the reponsibility to humanize the organization. If the employee has highly developed communication skills, the human contact can relieve the fear and sometimes the anger of a customer who feels overwhelmed with the computerized nature of most businesses. The time when your monthly bills came from familiar community members who could easily explain them is past. Today your bills are printed by computers three states away, and your inquiries are answered by another computer if not lost altogether in the existing maze of channels. An employee who is genuinely warm and who treates you as important and valuable to their organization, creates more good will than all the slick public relations departments in the world. One of the authors overheard a conversation on the phone recently during a convention. One of the conventioneers asked for the manager of the convention hotel. When the manager answered, the person described the kind action of a warm and accommodating desk clerk during a frantic check-in time the night before. His closing comment was, "I hope you value that employee as much as you should, because he creates more good will for you than all the elaborate advertising campaigns you can buy." The night clerk humanized the organization.

However, there is another facet of interaction involved in this responsibility. Within the organization, there are frequently needs for personalizing the system. Rules, new mandates, and policies that affect your subordinates can be made more acceptable if you, at a managerial level, can interpret them and explain them effectively. The ability to establish meaningful intra-company communication can create a personal touch. In turn, this perceived attitude can win employee loyalty and acceptance where frustration and conflict might otherwise grow.

Promoter

Employees are also important in promoting businesses. This promotion comes in overt, deliberate communications to audiences about the work and contribution of the business. It also comes in the employee's positive attitudes about the business which are projected to others. This does not mean that employees accept unquestioningly every policy and practice of an organization. However, any criticism should be, for the most part, constructive. Employees should be actively involved in problem solving, not problem creating.

Employees who promote their business will be on the receiving end, eventually. A sense of pride and accomplishment at being part of an enterprise which has the respect and admiration of a community is a worthwhile reward. Businesses that have earned the loyalty of their community are also usually prosperous businesses, and that prosperity is usually shared with those in its employ.

In each of these functions—interpreter, humanizer, and promoter—the core assumption dictates that the employee will have the ability to communicate effectively in order to accomplish that set of goals. Research has identified and isolated the particular communication skills that business demands.

Communication Demands of Business

General Competencies

It might seem simple to identify skill areas needed by those in the business world. However, a great amount of research has been conducted in order to identify these elements. Because the findings are important, we believe it is appropriate to examine them in some detail.

One important study and review of the literature was done in 1976 by three communication teachers. Their research focused on the person entering today's business organization and the skills that person should have. The study looked at communication with superiors, subordinates, peers within his or her own work group, and with those outside the work group. The study concluded that there are seven communication skills most important to that person's level of success. These were, in the order of priority: listening, advising, routine information exchange, small group problem solving, instructing, persuading, technical presentations.[4]

The authors point out, "The individual entering today's business organization must function in a dynamic communication system, and to some extent, the ability to function effectively in that communication system may determine perceived competency and level of success."[5]

Another 1976 study investigated the attitudes of training personnel. According to this study, the training personnel felt that the communication skills necessary for business success, arranged in order of their importance, were: listening, writing, interviewing, group discussion, reading, public speaking, non-verbal.[6]

Perhaps the most conclusive study, however, was published by Michael S. Hanna two years later. This survey dealt with the perceptions of top company executives, who identified eleven skills of communication which they had observed as troublesome or problematic for their employees. The company executives identified, in order of needs, the following communication skills: listening, motivating people, giving directions, delegating authority, group problem solving, handling grievances, private conferences (one-to-one), using the grapevine, formal presentation, conference leadership, negotiating and bargaining.[7]

However, Hanna discovered that these competencies are ranked somewhat differently when the list identifies those *used* most frequently by different levels of employees.[8]

Rank	*Managers*	*Supervisors*	*Labor*
1	Private Conference	Private Conference	Private Conference
2	Phone	Group Meeting	Group Meeting
3	Memo	Phone	Phone
4	Group Meeting	Memo	Memo
5	Letter	Letter	Letter

It is worth noting that, according to this study, the skills of *oral* communication are ranked highest and used most. In fact, the executives indicated that "71% of the company executives believe their employees are not good at giving feedback to supervisors; 54% say supervisors do not know how to get feedback, and 75% say that managers have a problem in getting and using feedback."[9] Yet, it is in this particular communication skill that company function and morale are involved.

The three studies cited here are typical of numerous others that clearly indicate the importance of oral communication. They further show that those entering the business world frequently lack adequate training in the use of these skills. These findings, however, are general. A look at some specific career areas will reinforce the importance of oral communication skills in business.

Some Specific Applications

Countless opportunities exist within every job and at every level of responsibility in the business and professional world to exercise the responsibilities we have discussed. It might be useful to look at some specific examples from among selected business situations in which you will be given a chance to use communication skills.

Retail. This broad term covers a lot of territory and a wide variety of job situations, from the gas station attendant to the grocery stock boy; from the clothing salesman to the jewelry consultant; from the credit manager of a department store to the check-out clerk in the local supermarket. But the common element that all of these individuals and thousands more share is that they deal directly with a customer who comes into a place of business in search of a particular purchase. Rarely is this person's main responsibility to make a sales pitch. Rather, the communication thrust from this perspective is usually to interpret for the customer the symbolization of menus, price lists, or store diagrams. Interpersonal skills are important, and attitudes that humanize the organization are vital.

Service. Persons involved in service industries especially need business speaking skills. Unfortunately, they are often the ones who lack them most. Since a service is involved, the establishment of credibility, or trust, is important in service industries such as repairmen, plumbers, electricians, and automotive mechanics. Research indicates that the high wages of such individuals are rarely resented or resisted if there is a feeling of confidence in the service person's work. Individuals employed in the service industry need skills to build a picture of competence and confidence and to communicate that image to the customer.

Medical. Although the TV picture of fatherly Dr. Welby is probably not the ideal, research indicates that those in the medical field need to upgrade communication skills and that the effect of bad communication can actually be health endangering. Doctors diagnose, and in so doing convey by both verbal and nonverbal messages their impression of the seriousness of the illness at hand. Medical personnel are sometimes called on to witness in court and must be able to present themselves well. Researchers must sometimes present the results of their research to lay persons as well as to fellow professionals. Medical personnel deal with the average person in periods of stress, sometimes extreme. Consequently, they need to be aware of how stress affects communication perception, and to be trained to overcome it through effective face-to-face communication techniques.

Industrial. Workers and management in industry are faced with many communication situations in the everyday course of the job. Another communication situation that is most important is management/labor negotiations. Although the labor unions employ professional negotiators for annual contract situations, frequently, the grass roots membership becomes a part of group decision making and of reporting to management.

Governmental. Governmental agencies are deeply enmeshed in a complex bureaucracy that calls for effective communication. Governmen personnel interpret mandates, explain the use of forms, and attempt to allay resistance or fear as an everyday part of employment. Insensitivity and defensiveness create problems rather than solve them. Yet, too often these are the responses given by those in governmental agencies to citizens. The result is impersonal if not hostile communication.

Educators. The educator is involved in every form of communication, and effective teaching depends on effective communicating. Unfortunately, teachers and professors are often deficient in these skills, particularly when they are required to speak outside the safety of their classroom. In this time when all levels of public education are under severe criticism by the community at large, those involved in education must develop more communication skills. If you are a teacher (or if you are training to become one), do not assume that you will only communicate to the students you plan to instruct. You will have many opportunities to speak to community groups, parents, and the administration.

Management. Communication skills in management are especially important, for managers must be skillful in speaking to subordinates, to superiors, and to the general public. They will often serve as spokespersons for the company in negotiations, in litigation, and in public appearances. A study by Meister and Reinsch in 1978 concluded, "In order for first-line managers to be promoted into middle and upper management, they must master fundamental management skills and activities. Communication is one of these skills."[10] This same study showed that first-line managerial personnel were perceived to have deficiences in the following areas: 50% in listening, 42% in management/employee relations, 42% in writing, 36% in problem solving, 31% in leadership, 25% in decision making, 23% in speaking, 19% in conference techniques.[11]

Law Enforcement. Men and women involved in law enforcement are highly involved in the use of communication skills. According to Erickson, Cheatham, and Haggard in 1976, "Researchers suggest that approximately 90% of police work involved communication activities not directly related to enforcement or crime prevention."[12] The same survey revealed that up to 72% of a police officer's workday is spent in some form of communication activity; 60% of that time with the public and 40% of that time within the department. Also, almost 100% of those situations involved conflict and stress. A group of police chiefs was surveyed to identify the skills necessary to meet this heavy communication demand on law enforcement officers. Seventy percent of those surveyed selected the following group of skills:

Listen Objectively
Public Speaking
Interpersonal Skills
Interviewing
Public Relations
Report Writing[13]

Summary

One researcher concluded her study of the use of training in business for human relations by stating, "In business, people have problems to solve, tasks to accomplish, goods to produce, and people to help. On-the-job communication is a major factor in accomplishing work and should be viewed primarily from this perspective."[14] As we have seen, the business community is a unique communication environment. Business has certain characteristics and needs that make communication training vital to those who would succeed. The nature and type of that communication training are important to understand.

The Nature of Communication Training

Productive Training for Special Needs

Research shows that the skills of oral communication are essential for success in the business world. We also know that within that environment, we are asked to communicate across many types of relationships and within many structured organizational systems. If we were to try to meet all those responsibilities without taking advantage of the results of study by the discipline, we would be foolish. If we fail to train for skills on the theory that they are "natural" and cannot be learned, we are equally foolish.

Communication Apprehension. The first reason training is necessary involves the nature of people and the communication process. Anytime you attempt to present your ideas or your position orally to others, you take a risk; you are vulnerable. If you write something down and others disagree or misunderstand, then they ususally do so out of your physical presence. Thus, you are removed from the moment of rejection. You have a buffer of space or time in which to recover. Or, you can comfort yourself by blaming their lack of intelligence with their inability to interpret what you have written.

However, when you speak face-to-face and there is misunderstanding or rejection, then you have the opportunity to try to clarify. If understanding is not reached, then the failure is more obviously yours. If there is disagreement with your plans, ideas, or opinions, you must face that rejection personally and immediately.

It is this element of risk in the oral communication process that creates communication apprehension, or what we commonly refer to as "stage fright." Ironically, the very characteristic of oral communication which makes it the most effective of all forms of communication is the physical and mental interaction between sender and receiver. It is also the most threatening of all forms.

"Beginning speakers can take comfort from the knowledge that the phenomenon we call stage fright is not peculiar to certain people, nor even to certain groups of people. The reactions occur in athletes, actors, musicians, teachers, and speakers. In short, they occur in anyone who is confronted with a situation in which the performance is important and the outcome uncertain."[15]

Because the element of risk is common to all communicators, experienced or beginning, so the presence of apprehension or fright is common to all. However, the degree of that anxiety is not common, nor are the means of coping with it. A great deal of research has been done in this area, but the research we will cite addresses itself to the effect of severe communication apprehension on people in the business environment.

James McCroskey and Virginia P. Richmond, in a comprehensive examination of this particular area, define communication apprehension as "an individual's level of fear or anxiety associated with either real or anticipated communication with another person or persons."[16] When that anxiety is abnormally high, communication effectiveness is inhibited. Usually the victim avoids and withdraws from any involvement with oral communication. Research indicates that in the general population of the United States, high communication apprehension is present in 20%–40% of Americans. To the extent that what is true of Americans generally also applies to business people specifically, then 20–40% of those in the business community may suffer from high communication apprehension and thus avoid or withdraw from oral communication situations. As a consequence, McCroskey and Richmond conclude that these individuals have greater difficulty establishing and maintaining interpersonal relationships.[17] The result, in a business situation, is grave.

First, because apprehensive individuals talk less, they have less input into the decision making process and are *perceived* by their co-workers and their superiors as having "lower competence, lower leadership, lower attractiveness, and lower sociability than other people and to be less likely to be turned to for opinion leadership than other people."[18] Keep in mind that perception of these qualities may be equal to reality. Hence, high apprehension brings unfair penalty to those who suffer from it.

Not only do others hold lower opinions of those who are abnormally frightened of speaking, but also these individuals see themselves as less successful. They do not press for advancement, they have less job satisfaction, and they have poorer relationships with peers, supervisors, and subordinates."[19]

The businesses that employ such individuals pay a cost. "Not only are they likely to be less productive, but they are also more likely to leave or have to be dismissed and thus require an additional expenditure to train their replacements."[20] So, in terms of personal cost and economic cost, training to relieve abnormally high communication anxiety is a good investment. We want to emphasize that there can be great value in a normal amount of tension in a communication situation, as long as the amount is not so abnormally high as to block your ability or willingness to engage in communication. In fact, normal apprehension can add alertness and awareness to a communicator and make the difference between a lackluster presentation and a memorable one. Your goal as a speaker is not to lose all anxiety, but rather to use it for positive results.

With that in mind, now let us examine the kinds of training which can be valuable to both those with severe communication apprehension and to those with average amounts of stress about communication.

Severe. Dr. James McCroskey's research offers the basis for understanding and treating speakers with high communication anxiety. The first step is to determine if your anxiety is abnormally high. This can be done very easily through a combination of two methods. First of all, you can simply be honest with yourself about your own history of behavior in the face of communication situations that are important to you and have an uncertain outcome. If you have consistently been immobilized by fear or dread, then you have a good reason to suspect that your communication apprehension is severe. A second method to determine this judgment is to use the Personal Report of Communication Apprehension, a paper-and-pencil test.[21] This instrument has been validated through extensive research and can give you some objective insight into your reactions.

If you determine that you have a severe degree of apprehension, you need to investigate and avail yourself of the training which has been developed to cure that response. This training is referred to as "systematic desensitization" (SD).

SD training is not a clinical psychology treatment, nor is it necessary for a business to spend a great deal of money to set up training sessions. The primary things needed are a quiet, relaxing atmosphere (such as a lounge area), a tape recorder, a deep relaxation instructional tape, and a qualified trainer (who could even be a layman). The sessions simply involve listening to the taped instructions and reacting candidly to the level of anxiety that you feel at specified points in the process. SD enables you to detect your anxiety and to understand its causes. Most importantly, SD helps you increase your level of calm and poise in a communication setting. Usually a group of 5–7 individuals can go through the training together. An average of 5 one-hour sessions has proven sufficient for all but the most extreme cases. Interestingly enough, the research has also shown that the results are long lasting, increasing the importance of taking such training as soon as possible.[22]

Materials such as the training tapes, the Personal Report of Communication Apprehension, details of setting up training sessions, and names of trainers who could assist in your locality can be obtained through Dr. James McCroskey of West Virginia University, or through the Speech Communication Association in Falls Church, Virginia. The important thing to remember is that a "properly administered program of systematic desensitization for communication apprehension will provide significant benefits to those involved."[23] Further, such a program is possible for any business or industry to implement with nominal expenditure of funds.

Normal. It may be that your personal history and the use of the PRCA lead you to know that your nervousness in communication situations is average, and not severe enough to require such elaborate methods of correction. If that is the case, your goal is simply to learn a few basic mental and mechanical techniques to control and use tension to your own benefit.

First, consider the mental state most productive for communication. Recall that we have already identified that before "stage fright" occurs, two elements must be present. First, you must perceive the outcome of the anticipated communication activity as important; and second, you must consider that outcome to be uncertain. Two things are necessary for you to control your anxiety.

First, you need to evaluate the importance of the outcome realistically. Certainly, any time you present a report, a sales presentation, or engage in a staff meeting, the outcome is important. However, it has been the authors' experience that individuals often exaggerate the importance of that outcome by failing to put the event into a proper perspective. It may be that your boss has left you the impression that "your job is on the line." You need to evaluate the event objectively and arrive at a rational decision of whether that is true or not. He or she may simply have been engaging an extreme motivation exercise, or he or she may have blown the event out of proportion. This is not to say that you should discount the importance of something without grounds, but careful and realistic appraisal may ease your anxiety.

Second, reduce the stress in your communication situations by reducing the uncertainty of the outcome. Two important steps will ease this uncertainty. Initially, realize that you do not have to be perfect. That may sound too simplistic, but it has been our observation in years of teaching speech that beginning speakers often assume that they must sound like Patrick Henry, be as effective as Billy Graham, receive the adulation of a Franklin Roosevelt, and be as entertaining as Bill Cosby, or forever face the stigma of failure! What a ridiculous and impossible standard to set for oneself! Failure is insured by this kind of thinking. Instead of expecting a standing ovation for your performance, adopt as your standard the time-proven measuring stick of communication—"Was I effective?"

One insurance of effectiveness in the business world is to follow the suggestions and steps outlined later in this book for the particular kinds of communication in which you are involved. Another is to remember that each time you present material orally, you will be making improvement over the time before. Ultimately, gaining experience is the best method for overcoming the problems of tension. And finally, remember that you will not be competing to reach perfection, but simply to get your message across.

With that in mind, the second thing you can do to reduce the uncertainty of outcome is to prepare thoroughly and to practice. In any human activity whatsoever, we do not expect to be able to perform effectively unless we have prepared and rehearsed our effort. Yet, people often approach a speech situation with little or no preparation and expect to be successful. That attitude is unrealistic. Conversely, there are other people who dread the communication event, no matter how well prepared they are. That attitude is unnecessary. Careful preparation, using every available source of assistance, and several practice sessions can give you a great deal of self confidence; and they should go a long way toward relieving uncertainty.

But, you may say, "I have prepared and practiced, and still I have been horribly frightened." We would agree that is possible. Remember, you will always have an element of fear. But that is not necessarily bad! There are some mechanical things which you can do that will give you physical relief. It is important to remember that although the state of stage fright is almost entirely psychological, the symptoms are totally physical. One of your first goals should be to build some deliberate activities into the pre-speaking and speaking times to help you use up the excess energy with which your body is supplying itself.

In the initial planning stages, remember to include deliberate activities as an integral part of the presentation. Use visual displays that will require your moving across the room, arranging slides or pictures, distributing charts and graphs to the group, or drawing or writing on a chalkboard. Plan a demonstration for one part of the speech in which you demonstrate or act out what you are talking about. You will feel comfortable showing others how to do whatever you may feel very uncomfortable just talking about. Plan some points of deliberate interaction with you audience. We do not refer here to just the usual, "Are there any questions?" at the conclusion of your speech. We refer more specifically to times in the speech when you ask members of the audience for a response, or in which you invite them to assist you in formulating something. This give you a chance to focus attention briefly on someone else. It shares the spotlight which may have become too intense for you. Keep in mind the first sentence of this paragraph, "in the initial planning stages." Until you become highly experienced, it is better not to try extemporaneous departures from your planned presentation. They might not be executed well. A sudden call for "a volunteer from the audience" to assist with an integral part of your speech may produce no response or an unpredictable one. However, if you plan such activities as suggested here and you rehearse them, you can give yourself mechanical help in relieving the static energy coursing through your body and creating physical reactions such as dry tongue, shaking hands, sweaty palms, and quaking knees.

Finally, we suggest one last positive mental response to the symptoms of communication apprehension. It has been absolutely established that they are never fatal! You will not die from giving a speech, but if you have trained and have worked at taking remedial actions to ease those symptoms, it is almost certain that you may well live easier and more profitably.

Managerial Skills. Another area in which training in communication is necessary is the development of successful leadership techniques and styles within organizations. There is a great body of literature in various professional journals regarding management styles. The particular style of leadership or management needed by a given organization depends on a large number of factors in that organization. Nonetheless, many different studies have shown that the kind of management that encourages the participation of employees, a certain amount of self-direction, attention to individual needs as well as organizational ones, will result in improved productivity, higher employee morale, and better decision making.

Some of the communication characteristics of effective managers have been identified. In a rather extensive review of the literature, Bradley and Baird point out that effective leaders "gave suggestions, asked questions, stimulated participation, encouraged alternative suggestions, and demonstrated a desire for the group to reach its own conclusion."[24] Another study showed effective managers "excelled in giving suggestions, addressing employees by name, and engaging in information exchange."[25]

These are not necessarily characteristics of communication which managers and organizational leaders naturally have. Training is necessary in order to develop these traits and to insure that the style of management within an organization is as effective as it can be.

The type of training for business leadership can also be provided by company policy and need. Many managerial consultants are available and can be brought in to train leaders on-the-job. Formal courses in the academic setting are useful. They can be found in departments of business, communication, and frequently in night courses offered through the college's division of continuing education. Self-study is possible. Reading a book such as this one, and genuinely attempting to increase communication along determined lines can help you to acquire the kinds of communication skills that help make you a superior manager.

Listening. J. Paul Lyet, chairman of Sperry Corporation, recently announced the corporation's commitment to improving the quality of listening among its 87,000 employees. He stated, "Poor listening is one of the most significant problems facing business today. Business relies on its communications system, and when it breaks down, mistakes can be very costly. Corporations pay for their mistakes in lower profits, while consumers pay in higher prices."[26]

Confirming Mr. Lyet's words are the studies that we looked at previously. Each of the three studies cited indicated that the most important communication skill needed in business was the skill of listening. The study conducted by Hanna in 1978 found that top executives "ranked listening as most troublesome or second-most troublesome . . . The implication that we should focus our instruction more heavily and directly on listening skills seems obvious."[27] Further, Sylvia Porter pointed out in the *Washington Star* in November of 1979 that individuals are generally aware of their deficiency in listening. "85 percent of those asked rate themselves as 'average' listeners or less, while fewer than 5 percent rate themselves as 'superior' or 'excellent'."[28]

Studies in listening indicate that after listening to a 10 minute presentation, the "average person has heard, understood, properly evaluated, and retained only half of what was said. Within 48 hours, that sinks another 50 percent."[29] So, the end result is that, on the average, we comprehend and retain only about 25 percent of what we hear. That can be even more alarming when we realize that as ideas are passed from one person to another, they can become distorted by 80 percent.[30]

These studies do not confine themselves to the business world. However, as Mr. Lyet pointed out, in the business setting, mistakes in listening are not only socially disastrous but also economically punishing. With 100 million workers in the United States, a simple $10 listening mistake by each one would cost business $1 billion![31] On a less global scale, consider business persons who listen poorly when their secretary tells them of an appointment. They may accidently make the appointment on time but come ill equipped to respond to the customer's inquiries, thus losing an account. They may miss the appointment altogether, thus not only losing an opportunity for a sale but creating a negative customer feeling toward the entire company. Or, they may be late and have to work harder to overcome the impression of rudeness and carelessness which their lateness has established.

The salesperson who glibly talks without responding to the customer's repeated non-verbal signals that he or she has a question may lose a sale without ever realizing that he or she has done so because of poor listening. The new employee who listens poorly will not follow the plain instructions which he or she has not heard. His or her job efficiency report will be negative, not because he or she lacks the skills to perform, but because he or she has not developed the skill of effective listening. The physician who is a poor listener may fail to pick up on the clues his or her patient gives him or her and therefore may misdiagnose the illness. A patient who fails to listen to the doctor's advice runs a risk to health and even life. Executives who fail to listen carefully to their subordinates may totally miss a decline of morale on their staff and never know they have a serious personnel problem which could be solved by good listening.

We know that listening plays an essential and important role in business communication as well as all other fields of communication. We know that listening and being listened to affect general emotional balance and mental health. "We know that the organizational policy of management, management's attitude toward keeping people informed, and the degree and type of participation in the organization all affect the place of listening within a business."[32] Importantly, we know that *listening can be improved by training.*

The type of training that you can use to improve your listening can be highly formalized or it can be basically a "self-improvement" study. We have such good available research on listening that it is possible to isolate characteristics of good listening. Let us turn to the authorities for suggestions for improvement.

Listening Roles. A major consideration in understanding the function of listening in the business environment is the impact of listener roles. The structured role set in which one is placed in a business organization influences the quality and the type of listening one does. Just as the purpose of a speech will determine its content and presentation, so will the particular role out of which you listen in a business communication situation determine the kind of listening that is effective. The factor that complicates this and creates problems for the listener in business is the constantly shifting nature of the roles in which one is placed.

As a business person, you must be prepared to listen in the roles of subordinate, peer, superior, and public representative. Each of them places you in a different listening posture.

When you listen as a subordinate, you primarily listen for orders and instruction. Consequently, the major role which you will fulfill is to be an information processor. The single goal you should have is to "get the facts." Habitual notetaking, questioning for clarification, paraphrasing for reinforcement, and reviewing instructions immediately following the close of the communication are the habits that will make you more effective in that listening role. Unless specifically invited by the one communicating with you, you should always view your listening role as a subordinate, or a data recipient.

There will be other times when you will listen as a peer. Peer roles offer opportunities for direct interaction with one or more associates. The communication goal may be to share information, to reach mutual decisions, to make cooperative plans, or to engage in problem solving. The key to peer listening is to get the full information, but also to be a team member who will need to react to the information received. Thus, you will be an evaluative listener, one who brings his or her own experiences, observations, and opinions to bear on the material under consideration.

The third role that you will occupy as a listener is that of superior. In this role, you function primarily to gather feedback. Your attitudes in this role make the difference in whether or not you get the feedback necessary to understand potential problems areas, to evaluate progress, and to access future plans. An authoritarian, judgmental attitude in this role discourages feedback. What you do receive from subordinates will lack honesty, since your subordinates will tell you only what they think you want to hear.

Your final role as a business person listener is the role of public representative. In this role you may listen a great deal over the phone. You may listen to customer complaints and inquiries. You may discuss sales plans with a potential customer, or you may talk about your company with other company executives. Whatever the situation, you listen for the purposes of discovering knowledge of the market, spotting opportunities for you and your company, and sampling public opinion. The most important attitude you should cultivate in this role is sensitivity. Listen to what you are being told, as well as what you can sense. This listening role is one of having your "ear to the ground." You seek knowledge which others do not necessarily want to give you directly. If you are blissfully unaware of the unspoken messages sent your way, you may be miserably aware of lost opportunity later.

Because the person involved in business has unique roles to fulfill in listening, the special responsibilities of each of those listening roles must be fully understood. Once they are grasped, you can look at the literature concerning listening in general and apply the standards of effective listening to each of the particular roles you may be fulfilling.

Listening attitudes. Although writers use many different terms and frameworks for describing the characteristics of effective listening, most of the literature can be formulated under four basic attitudes.

First, good listening requires *effort*. When people say that listening is easy for them, they may be saying that they aren't doing a very good job. Listening is active, not passive. Good listening means total involvement, both mentally and physically. Constant eye contact, non-verbal feedback, and close attention are necessary for total listening. For the subordinate, these practices are necessary to absorbing the data. But for the superior, they are equally important in making the subordinate you are listening to feel that he or she is being heard and that his or her opinion is valued. The listener who merely endures others' speaking time, and uses it mainly as a preparation period for his or her own next speaking performance, is not giving sufficient effort to accomplish good listening.

Good listening requires *empathy*. A listener who hears and is sensitive not only to the facts, but also to the feelings and ideas of the speaker, is one who listens with empathy. This kind of listening might be called "listening between the lines." One writer has called it the ability to listen to what is not being said. An empathic listener not only comprehends the feelings of the speaker; this listener encourages and gives positive feedback to the speaker. This does not necessarily imply that the speaker's feelings are shared or that you will refrain from registering opposite opinions. It means that the way you listen allows the other individual to feel secure in sharing his or her ideas with you. As a superior and as a peer this is an especially vital attitude to cultivate. Many labor relation problems could be avoided, lessened, or resolved by empathic listening between the negotiators.

Patience is also required for effective listening. Patience means more than just affording an adequate amount of clock time for the communication, although this is certainly part of the process. Patience also means reserving judgment in order to enable the speaker to complete a presentation before you register a reaction. In the role of superior, your impatience can effectively stifle the creativity and initiative of your subordinates whose ideas are rejected before they are fully explained. As a subordinate, a lack of patience can cause you to react prematurely to a directive before you fully understand its complete impact.

Finally, if you are to be a good listener, you approach communication situations with *curiosity*. Every communication has a purpose. If you are to listen appropriately, you must question in order to clarify. There has to be an attitude of selfishness in good listening.

In essence you say, "I will listen so that anything that may benefit me, I will hear." When you listen with curiosity, you are constantly calling for the "why," or the "how" of what is being discussed. You are preparing your own mind to hear and to assimilate information because you have been actively curious to have that data. In the lower grades of school, teachers often speak of a state of "learning readiness," referring to the time when the new first grader has enough accumulated experience to begin the word attack skills that will help him read. In our present context, we speak of "listening readiness," meaning the psychological attitude that prepares you to hear because you want to absorb what the other person is saying.

Listening conditions. We have identified the unique listener roles that business imposes on you. We have seen that all listening (no matter in what context) requires some common characteristics. In view of these facts, individuals can be trained to be better listeners. There are many commercial training sessions in listening, some of which are more valuable than others. You can obtain training in listening in the formal academic classroom or in the business training session. And, as is usually the case, you can improve your own listening ability if you use some relatively simple but somewhat demanding ground rules for improvement.

Harold Zelko and Frank Dance give the following list of suggestions in their book, *Business and Professional Speech Communication:*

1. Reduce distractions . . . we should try to eliminate or reduce distractions of any type. If the speaker is short on volume, we should move closer, turn off the fans, or do whatever else is necessary to cut out external noise.
2. Reduce emotional barriers . . . If we are emotionally overwrought and tense, it is difficult for us to attend to a speaker. . . . We should try to resolve as many of our own personal conflicts as possible before setting out to do a serious job of listening to an important subject.
3. Develop an attitude of wanting to listen.
4. Identify with the speaker and the speaker's message.
5. Apply the speaker's comments to your personal needs, wants, and interests.
6. Watch the speaker.
7. Organize what we hear.[33]

These techniques may seem to be simply common sense. However, the main assumption that each is built on is that you want to become a better listener. If that is true, then training in listening will result in your becoming a better practitioner.

Notes

[1] Vincent DiSalvo, David C. Larsen, and William J. Seiler, "Communication Skills Needed by Persons in Business Organizations," *Communication Education,* 25 (Nov. 1976), p. 270 and Janis E. Meister and N. L. Reinsch, "Communication Training in Manufacturing Firms," *Communication Education,* 27 (Sept. 1978), p. 243.

[2] Meister and Reinsch, p. 238.

[3] Dr. Florence Seaman and Anne Lorimer, "Competition and Teamwork," *Sunday Woman,* April 13, 1980, pp. 16–19.

[4] DiSalvo, Larsen, and Seiler, p. 275.

[5] DiSalvo, Larsen, and Seiler, p. 270.

[6] James E. Wasylik, Lyle Sussman, and Robert P. Leri, "Communication Training as Perceived by Training Personnel," *Communication Quarterly,* 24 (Winter 1976), p. 34.

[7] Michael S. Hanna, "Speech Communication Training Needs in the Business Community," *Central States Speech Journal,* 29 (Fall 1978), pp. 167–168.

[8] Hanna, p. 171.

[9] Hanna, p. 170.

[10] Meister and Reinsch, p. 243.

[11] Meister and Reinsch, p. 241.

[12] Keith Erickson, T. Richard Cheatham, and Carrol R. Haggard, "A Survey of Police Communication Training," *Communication Education,* Vol. 25 (Nov. 1976), p. 299.

[13] Erickson, Cheatham, and Haggard, p. 303.

[14] Joanne Gurry, "Career Communication in the Secondary School," *Communication Education,* 25 (Nov. 1976), p. 311.

[15] Bert. E. Bradley, *Fundamentals of Speech Communication* (Dubuque, Iowa: Wm. C. Brown Co., 1978), p. 390.

[16] James C. McCroskey and Virginia P. Richmond, "The Impact of Communication Apprehension on Individuals in Organizations," *Communication Quarterly,* 27, 3 (Summer 1979), p. 55.

[17] McCroskey and Richmond, p. 56.

[18] McCroskey and Richmond, p. 57.

[19] McCroskey and Richmond, p. 58.

[20] McCroskey and Richmond, p. 60.

[21] The PRCA is published in an article by James C. McCroskey, "The Validity of the PRCA as an Index of Oral Communication Apprehension," *Communi-*

cation Monographs, 45 (Aug. 1978), pp. 192–203. It may be used in business training programs by payment of a nominal fee to the Speech Communication Association.

[22] James C. McCroskey, "The Implementation of a Large-Scale Program of Systematic Desensitization for Communication Apprehension," *The Speech Teacher,* 21, 4 (November 1972), pp. 260–264.

[23] McCroskey, p. 264.

[24] Patricia Hayes Bradley and John E. Baird, Jr., "Management and Communicator Style: A Correlational Analysis," *Central States Speech Journal,* 28 (Fall 1977), p. 194.

[25] Bradley and Baird, p. 195.

[26] *The Washington Star,* November 14, 1979, Sylvia Porter, "Poor Listening Is Big Problem for Businesses."

[27] Michael S. Hanna, "Speech Communication Training Needs in the Business Community," *Central States Speech Journal,* 29 (Fall 1978), p. 170.

[28] *Washington Star.*

[29] *Washington Star.*

[30] *Washington Star.*

[31] *Washington Star.*

[32] Harold P. Zelko and Frank E. X. Dance, *Business and Professional Speech Communication, Second Edition* (New York: Holt, Rinehart and Winston, 1978), p. 172.

[33] Zelko and Dance, pp. 172–176.

II External Business Speaking

Changing Nature of External Business Speaking

180°–that is the amount of change in the American business attitude towards leveling with the public since the last century. The American concept of business and management has changed, and there is increased intensity in marketplace competition. There are numerous signs of a growing concern on the part of business regarding communication with the general public. Recall the "all the market will bear" attitude of the railroad magnates of the nineteenth century, and the "progress is paramount" attitude of the mining interests of the same time. Little or no consideration was given by these ruthless businessmen to the attitudes or desires of the general public. Today, by contrast, oil companies devote millions of dollars to public service advertisements on television. These have no purpose other than to assure the public that their practices are ecologically positive. The telephone company designs advertisements that portray it as a humanistic, "people oriented" company. Major businesses send their management staffs to training seminars in public address. Chambers of Commerce across the country form speaker's bureaus for the express purpose of sending out representatives of the business community to present business interests in a positive light to the public.

Three factors operate as a cause in this area. First, the competitive atmosphere of today's economy makes it necessary for the business community not only to provide goods and services at a profit, but also to give that "something extra" to be more appealing to the consumer than similar products offered by competitors. Market research has found that one "something extra" effective factor is a personal approach to the public. This is best achieved by skilled speakers who can present information and persuasion about the company and its practices.

A second factor that accounts for the importance and utilization of speaking in the community by business interests is the general shift in managerial philosophy that has occurred in the last fifty years. The autocratic, insensitive attitude which characterized business management of the nineteenth and early twentieth century has been replaced by an emphasis on employee participation and on input from the consumer.

This has been brought about, in part, by the move begun in the 60's of legislation that defines employee rights and litigation that has upheld the protection of those rights. No longer is the company immune to pressures from the public or attack by employees. Companies such as Southwestern Bell Telephone and millionaires such as the Hunt brothers have discovered that they can no longer operate in autocratic secrecy. Profit sharing plans for employees and information sharing plans for the public are equally important to labor and community relations for today's businesses and industries.

A third factor that has created a need for more public information has been the advent of unions, bureaucratic regulations, and consumer interest groups. These have combined to form a general movement toward management practices that depend on effective communication outside the company. Today's industries must constantly demonstrate their compliance with those regulations, and they must work at developing public support in fighting regulations that are too restrictive. The auto industry's resistance to air bags is a case in point. Although it has not made a change in the legislation yet, the public outcry against the Occupational Safety and Health Act (OSHA) is an illustration of the effectiveness of industrial rallying power among the public it serves.

General Principles of Public Speaking

What is a public speech? Although it might seem elementary, it helps to define terms before launching into a discussion of a concept. Public speaking differs from other communication settings in some important ways, but it also shares some basic elements common to most other types of human interaction.

Definition

Public speaking is communication, in which a speaker presents a fairly lengthy, prepared message, to an audience who have gathered for the purpose of hearing the message. All human communication involves a message presented from one person (called the source) to another person (or receiver) for some purpose. However, a public speech has some distinguishing characteristics that set it apart from the other methods of communicating.

Situation

The public speaking situation is an artificial situation. That is, everyone involved has to cooperate in creating the environment and atmosphere that makes it possible for a speaker to address a gathering. A time and place has to be set up, and everyone has to be in the right place at the right time. In other words, as a speaker, you address all of the audience members at the same time. You don't go around and tell individuals your message one at a time, at their convenience. That type of communication, the conversation or interview, also has its place in business. But an interviewer is not a public speaker just because he or she tells his or her message to many people—unless the people come together and make up a collective, simultaneous, live audience.

So, a public speech must be delivered in person by the speaker to the audience. That is what makes it *public* speaking. It is also what makes it scary, to all those speakers who contract a case of stage fright. Stage fright, or performance anxiety, is really a normal condition for almost all speakers, whether beginners or experienced.

Purposeful

The public speaking situation is purposeful. The speaker and the audience have a mutual purpose, which is related to the nature of the message to be given. The speaker wants to communicate a message to the audience for a certain, specific reason. Unless otherwise dictated, the speaker controls the purpose of the public speech, and that purpose may be to entertain the audience, to inform them, or to persuade them to a certain belief, attitude, or course of action. However, it is also true that the audience must agree to come together to hear the speech which is given for that particular reason. People who do not wish to be persuaded to a speaker's proposed purpose usually decline to attend the speech.

In the business world, of course, there are few speeches designed to simply entertain the audience, even though the most interesting speeches often contain elements of humor and enjoyment. What we usually see in business speaking is a message of some use or value to the audience in the job setting. Training lectures are in the category of informative speaking, as are sales reports and briefings. Sales pitches and motivational rallies are less informative, and more persuasive, since the main point is to get the audience to come to a given attitude or to take an action.

Length

A public speaking situation contains a fairly lengthy, prepared message or speech. By "fairly lengthy," we are drawing a comparison between the length of a public speech and the length of the comments passed between two people in a conversation, or among the members of a small group. In truth, all communication is prepared. Even in a conversation or a group discussion, you mentally prepare and rehearse your statements just prior to saying them to your receivers. You are able to do this without thinking in the few seconds during which the other person is speaking. Thus in communication theory, a public speech is not much different from one of the messages in the sequence of messages that pass back and forth between individuals in a conversation, or in a group discussion. The primary differences, of course, are that the public speech is much longer, by comparison, and the audience usually does not talk back. Consequently, it takes a correspondingly longer time for you to prepare and rehearse a public speech. There is no arbitrary set length of time that defines a public speech. In speech classes, we routinely assign students to present speeches as short as two or three minutes, to as long as ten minutes. On the other hand, Daniel Webster's famous "Reply to Hayne" in the U. S. Senate took about a day and a half for him to deliver. Today, we are accustomed to hearing sermons and political speeches of 20–30 minutes, and classroom lectures of an hour. Rarely do contemporary audiences sit still longer than that.

Delivery and Style

Whatever the length of the public speech—whether five minutes or one hour—people have some basic expectations of what it should be like. Your speech should deal with some specific topic or theme. In covering the topic, you organize the speech in a clear and logical manner. When you speak, you should begin with a relevant introduction, and conclude with an ending that satisfies the audience. Your language in the speech should be more formal and literate than in a casual conversation. You should eliminate vague pronouns, slang, and grammatical errors, however, the language should not be so formal that it is too complex or dull for the listeners. If you violate these and other basic audience expectations of a public speech, you will only frustrate the audience.

The audience also has some basic expectations of your delivery techniques. For instance, the audience expects you to use an audible volume in order for everyone to be able to hear what you say. You are expected to direct your comments to the audience in a personal, friendly fashion. When you fulfill that audience expectation, they cooperate by paying respectful attention to you. In line with a personal tone, the audience expects you to stand where they can all see you, to use eye contact and expressive emphasis, and to inject enthusiasm and force into your speech. In these and other ways, you meet the audience's expectations of at least the minimum delivery standards.

In summary, a public speech is a type of communication, in which you present a fairly lengthy, prepared message, to a group of people in an audience who have gathered for the purpose of hearing your message. It takes place in a special situation, where the audience members join together and cooperate in the speaker's purpose of succeeding in informing or in persuading. The degree to which the speaker's purpose is reached, i.e., how much information the audience learns, or how much persuasion takes place depends largely on how well you are able to meet the audience's expectations. What the audience expects is a unified, organized message. It should be related in interesting and understandable language, and delivered with a view towards effective communication.

This kind of communication might best be called "external." This would include all the contacts a business has with its public. Early in this century, large companies began to use extensive public relations departments to attend to these contacts. Today, management tends to see every employee of a business as influential in molding public opinion. Many companies expect all their employees to be well informed, to be adept at presenting the company to others, and to be able to "sell" the company's practices as well as its services and products.

Basic Considerations in Planning Public Speeches

There will be two major types of speeches that you may be called upon to give to an audience in some public setting external to your company. These are the speech to inform and the speech to persuade or influence. Each of these is a traditional form of public speech, but when adapted to the business setting, each has unique characteristics. Each type of speech is influenced in both content and delivery by the purpose that it has. At the same time, there are some basic steps in speech preparation regardless of the type of speeches you may be making.

Who Is the Audience?

One of the basic steps in speech preparation is the careful consideration of the audience. Audience characteristics such as age, sex, ethnic origin, socio-economic status, occupation, and numerous other identifying factors will have a great deal to do with your choice of subject, support, and delivery style. Imagine that you are going to represent your electric power company before the local high school, informing them about the actions your company is taking to bring about alternate energy sources. You would select different materials than if you were presenting a similar topic for the Company Board meeting, or for the annual National Convention of Electric Power Executives.

Another factor in understanding the audience is the set of attitudes that you can identify as belonging to the audience. Although it is impossible in most circumstances to know the specific attitudes of every member of your audience ahead of time, there are some clues that will be helpful. If the audience is a special interest group, such as the National Young Republicans Club, you can fairly well depend on their having a highly conservative, anti-big government attitude. So, if you are there to explain a new low income loan program for mortgages, you can expect some resistance to this additional government program. If the audience has no easily identifiable common interest, look for clues in the community. Knowing how the community voted in the last election, or what party the majority of the local citizens are from will indicate some broad outlines you can expect.

When you are contacted by a group to speak, or when your company sends you out on a speaking assignment, feel free to make inquiries about attitudes, opinions, size of audience, and any other background material needed so you feel more at home with the audience. Once you have isolated those audience characteristics, use them in the preparation and evaluation of your material.

Where and What Is the Occasion?

Understand your relationship to the occasion. This will give you some further indication of what is expected of you. If you are asked, for example, to speak about your company's recruiting policies to the local high school's senior class, you can safely assume that the occasion will be for the purpose of giving young people a chance to look over your compnay. If that same topic is requested for a meeting of the Citizens for Fairness in Employment, you may assume that the occasion will demand a more defensive position about your company's hiring policy.

Another important factor is the facility where you will speak. This is especially true if you plan to use visual aids. Check ahead of time on the availability of a screen, plugs of the type of your equipment requires, room lighting controls, and other important details. At a recent conference of educational consultants, a young women arrived in a somewhat hurried state and rushed to her room. She had brought a film which would last all but ten minutes of the one hour session. She discovered on arriving in the assigned room that the room could not be darkened, her three-pronged plug would fit none of the outlets, and there was no screen. She had planned to actually speak only ten minutes. Her presentation of sixty minutes was not a hallmark in public communication. Simple advance inquiries could have saved the day for everyone. Her discomfort was only exceeded by that of the audience who had to sit through the ordeal.

In line with the nature of the facility is the time factor. Never assume that you know how long you are to speak. One of the authors was recently contacted by the P. T. A. president and asked to "speak to the City Council of P. T. A. about the Fine Arts Program in our school district." She eagerly agreed to do so, assuming that she would have at least twenty minutes. As the conversation progressed and the president began to outline the other items on the meeting's agenda, it became apparent that she would have only a fraction of that time. A direct question was posed, and imagine her dismay to learn she was to tell about the total fine arts program of the district in "about two minutes."An immediate revision of the topic was offered to the president. The two minutes were used to discuss the art contest program conducted by the P. T. A. It is doubtful that even an experienced speaker could condense twenty minutes into two minutes without adequate warning.

What Can Be Told?

Know ahead of time the kinds of things which your company does not feel should be released to the general public. Your company may have a policy about prior approval of all speeches. If so, be sure that you follow the policy. You will want to clear anything ahead of time with your superiors. *This is especially true of information related to security or trade secrets.*

Where Is the Data?

Because you represent your company to the public, you need to determine what data is available, and where needed information can be found. Within the limits established by what you can talk about, make every effort to fill your speeches with concrete information. Try not to sound like you are simply delivering the "party line." Give your audience the feeling that they have been given some special insight into your company and its policies.

Once these general questions for preparation have been answered, you are ready to begin specific preparation for the speech. Because there are differences in the preparation approach for the speech to inform and the speech to influence or persuade, we will consider them separately.

Speaking to Inform

Steps in Preparation

In the speech to inform, "the speaker is an instrument of observation, like a camera, and an instrument of presentation, like a picture projector."[1] This representation of the speaker's responsibility in the speech to inform is intriguing, but oversimplified. Even in the straight informative speech, there are many decisions which the speaker must make.

Narrow Topic and Formulate the Specific Purpose Statement. When you are invited to speak on a topic to a group, you must formulate a statement of specific purpose. Contemplate the incongruity of speaking for five minutes on the exploration activities of the major oil company you work for. Merely naming off the drilling operations of the past week would probably consume more time than that. You need to take that broad topic (suggested in all probability by someone not very well informed about your company) and narrow it until you have a manageable topic. You may decide to speak on "Financial Risks Incurred in the Search for New Oil." Or another topic area might be "The Rise and Fall of a Dry Hole." Or you may want to inform the group about "Newly Discovered Oil in Your County." Whatever the approach you may want to take, you need to narrow your topic and formulate a specific purpose sentence. This sentence becomes your guide to the data you need and to the style of your presentation.

If you choose to talk about financial risks incurred in the search for new oil, your purpose sentence might be: "I will describe the financial risks incurred by Exxon in 1979 in the search for new oil in New Mexico." Or, you may want to use this purpose statement: "I will inform the audience about dry holes in the oil industry in a humorous fashion by describing in detail the frustrations and legalities of having a dry hole."

Notice that such a purpose sentence narrows the topic further, and indicates very specifically both the reasons for the speech and the manner in which you plan to accomplish it. You may or may not say that particular sentence to your audience of Kiwanians, Chamber of Commerce members, or whomever you are speaking to. However, if you fail to formulate that sentence for your own clarity, its absence will be apparent in the way you ramble through your speech.

Gather Information. We have already indicated the importance of knowing the location of data and its availability. Once you have set your specific purpose, you then seek the materials necessary to accomplish your purpose. When you limit your particular topic, as in the New Mexico exploration sentence above, you will need to find only that which is needed to support your particular purpose.

There are many different kinds of data that you should seek. Some suggestions might be:

- Personal Knowledge:
  - Observations and Experiences
  - Interviews
  - Surveys
- Published Knowledge:
  - Newspaper and Magazine Articles
  - Books on the Topic
  - Government Documents
- Company Documents

Organize the Speech. The methods for organizing a speech are some of the most important lessons to learn in our book. This skill alone is worth the purchase price of the book. Before launching on a systematic explanation of this crucial subject, let us pause to answer a few questions about it.

Q. Why do speech textbooks make such a big deal of an outline? Why does it matter if the Roman numerals and capital letters get mixed up?

A. This may come as a surprise to you, but most speech textbooks (including this one) do not overemphasize outlines. What we do try to stress is organization. Since a listening audience does not have a copy of your speech or outline to follow along, and since they cannot read your mind, organization is probably the most vital skill you can have as a speaker.

However, an outline is not the same thing as organization. It is merely a written diagram on a sheet of paper of your plan for the outcome of your speech.

Q. What is the first thing you write when you start composing a speech? Don't you begin with the introduction?

A. The first thing to write down is the purpose sentence, such as, "In this speech I intend to inform my audience that outlines are helpful to a speaker."

The next thing is to list several points supporting your purpose.

The list is not in final or complete form in its preliminary stage, but it starts your analysis rolling. It is best to remain with this task until you have a good list of topics with which to work. These topics form the basis for selecting the main ideas to be covered in the body of the speech.

For instance, we decided that outlines are important to a speaker for two reasons: they help you arrange the materials of your speech into a clear pattern, and they help you to see what is missing and might need further research.

After that, there are several things you can do. You can begin subdividing these points into their logical elements, plug in the supporting evidence you have, and work on the language.

The very last thing to prepare is the introduction. For example, Suppose you are at a party, and a boy asks you to introduce an attractive young woman to him. You say, "Sure. Miss, I'd like you to meet my friend, John Turkey. John, this is . . . this is . . . (Er, psst, what did you say your name was?)."

How can you introduce a speech until you know what you will say? How can you know that, until it is planned? Do the purpose first, then the main divisions, fill it in, and last of all, the introduction.

Q. What about the conclusion to the speech?

A. As Aristotle told us, there are three parts to a play or story, the beginning, the middle, and the end. Likewise, there are three parts to a speech, the introduction, body, and conclusion. Just as you have to have a way to get into the speech, you also have to get out of it in a manner that is more satisfying than, "Well, that's it."

The heart of the organization of a speech is how you arrange the main ideas, and how you support them with your evidence. The introduction and the conclusion are planned afterwards.

So let us begin our discussion of organization by looking at the body.

Outline the Speech. The body of the speech is made up of your main points or ideas, the explanatory sub-points that prove those main points, and the evidence or support for the explanatory sub-points. The main requirement for any speech to inform is that the audience know more about the subject when you finish than they did when you began. Thus, it is very important not only to give information, but to arrange it in a pattern or order that will make it clear.

There are a number of patterns of organization that a speaker may choose. The most common and useful ones are:

1. *Chronological*–This pattern divides the material according to a time sequence. What comes first, what comes next, what comes last?
2. *Geographical or Spatial*–This pattern divides the material by physical location. Divide an area into its regions, such as East, Central, West.
3. *Topical*–This pattern divides material according to broad subject areas. This is a logical analysis, not a "laundry list." The broad subject areas make up a complete idea, such as, "The federal government is made up of three branches, *executive, legislative,* and *judicial.*"
4. *Simple-to-complex*–This pattern is useful for presenting materials of a highly complex or abstract idea by first explaining the simpler components that make up its basis.
5. *Problem-solution*–Identifies a problem, analyzes the problem, established criteria for the solution, proposes a solution, evaluates a solution, and suggests implementation.

Your choice of which specific organizational pattern you use influences the kinds of materials you should select for your speech. You may want to attempt several organizational patterns until you find the one that you feel best spotlights the topic and presents it in the most logical order. One important thing to remember at this stage of preparation is that nothing you have decided thus far, except the decision to speak, must be kept. You may reach this stage of preparation and realize that your purpose statement is too broad or too narrow. Instead of feeling that you have to work within that original decision, this is the time for revision.

Once you are satisfied with the organizational pattern and supporting materials you plan to use, move into the preparation stage. During the speech construction itself, change becomes a little more difficult, although still not impossible.

The importance of an outline to a speech is twofold: an outline allows you to look at the entire presentation as a unit, and it identifies the areas that need more research or development. Unless you are enrolled in a class and required to hand in an outline, the outline is strictly for your use as a speaker. Consequently, because of its value, it should never be omitted.

The outline contains the main points, subpoints, and the supporting evidence for those subpoints. It shows the relationships between these elements of your speech. From the outline, you can identify areas that may need to be added, deleted, or strengthened.

Let us look at two sample outlines. The first represents a speech given by the manager of a local television station, speaking to a group of high school seniors on Career Day. When he was asked to speak about careers in television, he decided to limit that topic to television advertising. He chose to organize the speech in a *topical* sequence. (Note: the sample outlines shown here are for the *body* of the speech only. The introduction and conclusion will be explained later in this chapter.)

Sample Outline #1

Purpose Statement: To inform the high school seniors about a career in advertising with a local television station, Channel 9.

I. Television advertising has unique advantages over other forms.
  A. Television can demonstrate a product or service.
    1. Describe the Toyota advertisement.
    2. Show ski equipment television ad on videotape.
  B. Television can combine sight, sound, motion, and emotion.
    1. Compare magazine ad for Pepsi with television ad for Pepsi.
    2. Compare a newspaper ad for Luigi's Restaurant with television ad for Luigi's.
  C. Television can target the buying audience for a product.
    1. Describe the ad campaign for the last rock concert.
    2. Describe the ad campaigns for children's toys at Christmas.
II. Local stations derive most of their revenue from local ads.
  A. Commercials make up a large part of the schedule.
    1. Display station log book.
    2. Statistics: ads make up 15% of the broadcast day.
  B. Many ads are produced locally.
    1. Statistics: 60% of the ads are produced by the networks, but are "packaged" with the network show. 40% are local.
    2. Statistics: 1 1/2 minutes of local ads are shown for each 30 minute show.
    3. Statistics: 90% of the stations's spot sales are locally produced ads.
III. Local stations have high involvement in the ads.
  A. Ads made through an ad agency require some involvement by the local station.

1. Description of station's duties as producer.
2. Illustration of time required to meet those duties.

B. Ads made without an ad agency are total responsibility of the station.
1. Description of process for scripting.
2. Anecdote concerning crew.
3. Total production schedule for one ad.

C. This involvement calls for additional staffing by local station, i.e., jobs for you.

The second sample outline represents a speech given by the mayor of a small town following his return from a tour of the Soviet Union. His audience is the Junior Chamber of Commerce Auxiliary, the Jaycettes. His topic area is youth organizations of Russia, and his goal is to inform these women of the sequence of organizations that Russian young people move through. He organized the speech using the chronological arrangement pattern. Notice that this outline utilizes key words instead of sentences as the previous one did.

Sample Outline #2

Purpose Statement: To inform the Jaycettes of the sequence of Youth Organizations to which Russian young people may belong.

I. The Pioneers
  A. Membership
    1. Mandatory
    2. Age 6
  B. Activities
    1. Indoctrination, political
    2. Limited military training
      a. Anecdote: Pioneers marching demonstration
      b. Testimony: General's statement about importance of Pioneers

II. Communist Youth League, or Komsomel
  A. Membership
    1. High school, college
    2. Maximum age, 28
  B. Advantages
    1. Better jobs
    2. Contacts for future

C. Problems
   1. Testimony from Prof. X: "This age group produces some questioning of the Communist system; some individuals refuse to believe everything they are taught by the leaders."
   2. Statistics: number expelled from membership last year.

III. Communist Party
   A. Membership
      1. Competitive and strictly limited
      2. Young adults sometimes are members
      3. Standards and requirements
   B. Advantages
      1. Promotions
      2. Non-members from Pioneers and Komsomel

A careful look at these outlines will show the importance of deciding on the actual evidence that you will use to support your sub-points. The interest level of a speech depends on a variety of the forms of evidence, among other factors which we will discuss later. Note that in each of these speeches, there are plans for a variety of kinds of evidence.

Supporting the Main Points. This is a good time for us to look carefully at the sort of evidence that you should have gathered in an earlier preparation step. However, knowing the identity of the types of evidence as well as the strengths and limitations of each may well help you decide on what to use. Traditionally there are six different kinds of evidence that can serve as support. We will look at each of them separately.

Specific instances. This is a brief factual example. If you are trying to make the point that a young person at your local high school has many choices of subjects to take, a logical form of support would be to give examples of the different kinds of courses offered at each grade level. If your point is that more and more small businesses are acquiring their own computers, then a list of several local concerns who have bought them in the last year will establish your point.

Illustration. This form of support is actually an extension of the specific instance into a story. If you are attempting to prove that small businesses can utilize computers, you might want to take the case of one local businessperson and recount in some detail the experience he or she had in seeking and purchasing his or her own computer. An illustration is especially forceful when it is used in combination with statistics that establish that the illustration is not just an isolated example.

Comparison or analogy. Drawing a comparison between objects, persons, or events is called an analogy. The purpose of the comparison is most often to clarify or dramatize an area in which the two are alike. It is often used to help explain something which is abstract or highly complex. Traditional logicians always qualify analogies by stating that they do not prove but only clarify. However, analogies are useful supporting materials.

Statistics. Statistics are numerical facts. They may come in a variety of forms and within a wide range of acceptability. Statistics are the most impressive sounding of the forms of support, but they also can be misrepresented and are often difficult to detect if they are. You should be particularly cautious in the presentation of statistics from two aspects. First is the ethical aspect of being certain that the statistics are accurate, and that the inferences you draw from them are logical and valid. A second reservation is that large doses of statistics to an audience that is not accustomed to dealing with them will literally lose their interest, and thus be counter productive to your speech.

Testimony. A direct quotation from another person is considered testimony. Two very important things need to be recognized. First, testimony carries only as much weight as the individual you quote. Second, testimony, even from an expert, still represents someone's opinion, not necessarily a fact. We have heard long arguments between individuals regarding the veracity of some point of view, with the clinching argument being, "Well, it must be right because I have the testimony of X!" Students in competitive debate are often guilty of this kind of thinking, but a close look at newspapers and magazines will tell you that other people make the same error in thought.

Another factor to be aware of in offering testimony is that a high level of expertise in one area does not transfer as expertise in all areas. We are often inundated with asserted testimony from sources outside of their fields, designed to sway our opinion and influence our actions. A case in point is the use of movie stars and athletes to advertise everything from panty hose to automobiles. Scientists and scholars are often quoted in a political or a religious context, in which their credentials are very slim. When you find testimony for support in a speech to inform, be certain that the person you are quoting is one whose opinion *in that particular subject* area should be respected. Nevertheless, quoting a well-known person (especially an attractive person) serves you as interesting support, at least.

Visual aids. In business speaking, especially, we believe that visual aids are often needed. There are numerous types of visual aids that you can use, including models, pictures, overhead transparencies, slides, films, and videotapes. The primary advantage of visual aids is to give an additional dimension of sight (or sight and sound) to the oral presentation. As we have discussed elsewhere in this book, they often spark interest, alleviate stage fright, and create easier acceptance of abstract or complex concepts.

The main thing to remember when planning to use visual aids is that they are for the purpose of underlining and supporting the main ideas of the speech. If they are so complicated themselves, or their use is awkward, or if they cannot be seen easily, they may do more harm than good. In addition, the quality of the visual aid should be superior, particularly for the businessperson, because that can reveal (nonverbally) the level of value you have placed on your own presentation.

Plan the Introduction and Conclusion

Functions of the Introduction. Both of the sample outlines previously presented above lack two important parts, the introduction and the conclusion. Once you decide on the organization of your main points and define for yourself the types of supporting materials you want to use, you are ready to formulate a way to begin and end the speech. You need to exercise all the creativity that you can muster. In this part of the speech planning, you reach out to appeal directly to the audience and set the mood and the intent of the speech.

The introduction of a speech answers three unspoken questions from the audience. First, the audience might well ask, "Why should I listen to this speaker?" In the opening part of your speech, you must establish in some way that you have the authority, the experience, or at least the interest to equip you to speak to this audience. You do not need a direct statement establishing these factors. It may be set up through indirect reference, through material you are in a position to know, or through your own status in the community. The person who formally introduces you to the audience can often help you along.

The second unspoken question of your audience is "Why should I listen to this subject?" The first attempt to answer that question is upon chosing the subject. As we discussed, your analysis of the audience and its probable attitudes toward the subject should have been a part of your preparation. Now, as your formulate the introduction, you must tell the audience a good reason to listen to this subject. You need to reach out to their needs, their wants, their interests, their desires. Again, you may do so subtly, but you must establish a good reason at this point for them to hear what you have to say.

The last question the introduction of your speech should answer is, "What are we going to hear?" The formulation of the purpose statement is the first attempt you have made to deal with this question. When you formulate a transition between the introduction and the body of the speech, include a signpost of what is ahead. Think about the need for this totally oral activity to take a permanent place in the minds of your audience. The best way to insure that is to give the audience a preview of major points so that they can listen for the things that are ahead.

Techniques of Introduction. The most effective introduction to any oral presentation is one that reaches out from the speaker, through the subject, back to the audience and then joins those three elements of the communication situation. If you accomplish that, it is really irrelevant which technique you use to do it. However, we will examine five techniques that may be used for speech introductions.

1. *Direct Reference to Communication Elements.* The introduction for a speech may be built on a simple reference to the occasion, the speaker, the audience, or the topic. A direct reference may not be a "gimmick." It may not be dramatic, and it may not necessarily create laughter in the audience. It is, however, sometimes the most effective way to get a speech before an audience. Review the sample outline for the speech on Russian Youth Groups, and consider the following possible introduction, which would utilize this method.

"After returning to this country from the Union of the Soviet Socialist Republics, I am constantly reminded of the differences between the two nations. But perhaps nowhere do I see this more dramatically than I do as I contemplate the differences in the lives of Russian and American young people. I felt since you as Jaycettes are not only strongly proud of our nation, but also intensely interested in the lives of our youth that it would be appropriate this evening to discuss the organizations that Russian young people are involved in."

This introduction joins the audience, the speaker, the occasion, and the topic into a close and natural relationship. It leaves no doubt in the minds of the audience about what will be covered and why; yet it allows the speaker the comfort of a straightforward approach to his or her audience.

2. *Shocking Remark or Startling Statement.* This approach in the introduction can be highly effective and can certainly get the audience's interest. It is important, however, not to shock so completely that the audience is offended. Also, try not to create such a sensation with the introduction that the rest of the speech seems tame and rather boring in contrast. Consider for example the speech on careers in local TV advertising. The speaker might begin with:

"You don't have to go to New York to make it big in advertising!"

or

"You can make $30,000 a year in your first year of employment right here in Fort Worth, Texas."

A speaker attempting to dramatize the dangers of drugs might point to his student audience and say, "Four of the forty of you sitting here could be dead of drug abuse by tomorrow." Such a statement would have to be followed with the supporting statistical data, but it certainly is an attention-getter.

3. *Humor.* A humorous introduction is almost always effective. However, if you are the type of person who always forgets the punch line of a joke, or who simply can't tell one to your best friends and get a laugh, then you should not plan one for the introduction of your speech. The kind of humor that is usually most effective from the platform is a natural outgrowth of the situation or people involved in it, rather than a joke from "Capt. Billy's Whiz Bang" publication. However, humor is appreciated when it is done well. Clever turns of words or phrases are appropriate in combination with other primary techniques.

4. *Quotation.* Another appropriate way to begin a speech is to quote from a piece of literature, song, or famous person relating to the topic of your speech. If you use this method, give credit to the source. Formulate a transition sentence between the quotation and the body of the speech. For example, refer to the sample speech outline on careers in TV advertising (pp. 37–38). An introduction for that speech might be:

"Harry Truman was famous for the axiom he had framed on his desk in the White House which said, 'The buck stops here.' Now, Mr. Truman meant that he would be responsible for any decisions made by his administration. But when local TV stations say, 'The buck stops here', they mean that they are making the Big Bucks these days in the field of advertising."

5. *Hypothetical Illustration.* A hypothetical illustration is simply a fiction you publicly admit to. However, it is sometimes a very effective kind of introduction. The speaker who can spin a tale and get the audience involved in it can often lead them into a speech that they might otherwise have rejected. The ethical key is to be sure to designate that it is hypothetical. The speech about Russian Youth Organizations might be introduced as follows:

"I'd like you to know a young man from Russia, Ivan Dornski. Imagine with me for a moment that this 21-year-old man is standing here with us this evening. He would be dressed in modern clothes and would be a recent graduate of Moscow University. He would in every respect look very much like one of your sons or mine. But there would be a very real and very dangerous difference. Since the age of six, Ivan has been immersed in the strongest network of youth organizations that exists today. He has been indoctrinated and molded. He does not question, he does not hesitate. What the leaders of Russia ask, he is prepared to give. And there is a nation of Ivans in the Soviet Socialist Republic. This evening I would like to acquaint you with those organizations that mold the youth of Russia."

The introduction, therefore, is important for the purposes it serves. It establishes your right to speak, and the reason why the audience should listen to you. It tells the audience why the topic of the speech is worth their attention and prepares them to know what to expect in the course of your speech.

The introduction of your speech determines the initial reaction your audience has to that speech. It is the first direct contact you have with them. It is important and deserves careful planning and consideration.

Function of the conclusion. By the same token, the conclusion is the last impression that an audience has of you and your speech. It has been said that it is far more difficult to stop talking than to get started. Often speakers fail to give enough consideration to their conclusion. It should be dynamic, impressive, and obviously well thought out. Any of the techniques suggested for introductions can also be used in the conclusion. The determining factor is that the conclusion should do just that—it should conclude. It should have a feel of completeness, and should leave the audience with the single impression or idea you have been trying to get across to them.

Techniques of the conclusion. Restatement, summary, and completion of the idea begun in the introduction can be effectively used in the conclusion of a speech to inform. A good way to visualize the conclusion is that it should "tie the bow" on the package that has been your speech. It should never consist of a desperate look, a shrug of the shoulder, and the helpless murmur, "Well, I guess that's all."

Consider, for example, a conclusion for the Russian Youth Organization speech, which we illustrated as beginning with the hypothetical example of Ivan. You might conclude that speech in this manner:

> "Thus for life, the young people of Russia, the Ivans and Katrinas are enveloped in an effort by that nation to make committed citizens of them. Though we may not embrace the ideology, we cannot help but be impressed with the methodology."

Having formulated the introduction and the conclusion of your speech, you have now completed the preparation phase in terms of the mental planning. It is now the time for your physical preparation step.

Practice the Presentation. Regardless of your level of experience in public speaking, practice is essential. Up to this point, the speech is a product of your imagination. It exists only in your mind. But if it is to be effectively delivered, it must exist in the language of oral presentation. The only way that this can happen is through oral practice.

The more complex your delivery plans are, such as the use of visual aids, the more imperative it is that you practice, preferably in the facility where the speech will be given. This is not always possible, however, so you need to find a place where you can practice without disturbing or being disturbed. Use a video or audiotape recorder to practice, if such equipment is available. Get a trusted friend to listen and make suggestions.

One important reason for practicing orally is to get an idea of how much time you will need for what you have planned. Timing a speech in practice is never exact—you invariably present the speech "for real" to the audience at either a faster or a slower pace. However, you will know whether your speech is significantly under or over the time limits that will prevail. It is best to learn that fact in a harmless rehearsal, while you still have an opportunity to revise your plans.

Whatever method you decide to use for practice, be sure you do *practice.* Experiment with various wordings, check your speaking notes, and do everything to assure yourself that you will be comfortable when the moment comes to make the actual presentation. Assure yourself that you have done everything possible to make a successful showing.

Speaking to Influence

Overview of Persuasion

The basic purpose of every communication act is to accomplish a specific response from another individual or group. For the most part, human communication aspires to influence in one way or another. Even when we give a speech to inform, at the core of our purpose is a desire to influence the audience's thinking because we have added to their body of knowledge or changed their perception of some facet of life. David Berlo said, "In short, we communicate to influence."[1]

There are times, however, when the primary focus of the communication act is to change the audience's position to one more nearly like our own. Clearly, this kind of communication is for the purpose of directly persuading or influencing. Sales presentations in the business world are the primary type of influencing in which business speakers engage. But often, the business speaker is called into the community in a different, external communication context. In this situation, the purpose is to influence the audience's position, opinion, or actions with regard to the institution of the business. This differs from a routine sales pitch to the audience as consumers of the goods and services supplied by the company.

Such activities by business have increased in recent years to the extent that some major universities now offer specializations in corporate advocacy. Even those businesses and industries that do not employ a person specifically for such a position expect that those involved in their company fulfill that responsibility. You will be inextricably identified with your business. The image you project of the actions and philosophies of your business will be accepted by the larger community as one measure of their value.

Business depends on its employees to translate the company's actions and concerns outward to the public. By the same token, those employees play a part in the process of interpreting the public's needs and motives inward to the company. The company's representatives are expected to "read" such interactions and to marshal public support, whether national or local in scope, for the specific policies and actions of that company.

We assume here that business persons are informed and aware of the company's vested interests. The main need is for you to acquire skills of composition and presentation for oral communication. Our aim is to help you develop the ability to be an effective corporate advocate.

A large corporation recently contracted to purchase land as the site for a new, gigantic shopping mall. This area of town had recently been developed with expensive homes, and the residents were deeply distressed. Immediate petitions were circulated, law suits were contemplated, and city council meetings were besieged with irate homeowners who were convinced that the mall would irreparably damage their property values.

The ensuing public forum created a ready-made arena for representatives of the corporation, as well as the stores that had contracted to move into the mall. Civic clubs, town meetings, and even churches invited members of these businesses to explain what steps would be taken to avoid a general downgrading of the property in the area. Had these businesses not been equipped to answer this need, the investment of literally millions of dollars could have been lost.

Arthur Schlesinger made the point most clearly when he stated, "If man or mechanism were infallible, there would be no need for persuasion; but because they are not, the discipline of consent is indispensible to civilized society."[2] Because business is not infallible, and because it is often on the cutting edge of civic change and controversy, the ability to speak in order to influence the general public is an important skill to acquire.

Sources of Persuasion. Since the time of Aristotle, professionals in the field of speech communication and rhetoric have attempted to analyze and prescribe successful persuasion. There is a body of literature that attempts to determine which is more influential in the persuasive process, logic or emotion. For our purposes, we will take the position that logical and emotional appeals are equally influential in persuasion. Anyone who aspires to influence others through oral discourse must be prepared to offer both. Further, we believe that in the business world, there is a third element of persuasion, which we will refer to as status.

Logic. Man is influenced through the use of logic. An individual has some mental or intellectual conviction to act in a certain way. This does not mean that it will necessarily be sound, nor even that the person can verbalize that mental process. But thought is the predecessor of action, even when the thought is not clearly understood. The speaker who would influence another must be prepared to use logical appeals and to offer not only the facts, but an explanation of the facts.

1. *Explanation.* A number of authorities suggest that one of the most effective persuasive forms is persuasion by explanation.[3] This occurs when you offer the audience what appears to be simply a set of facts and an explanation of them. These are *selected* facts that have led you to reach the conclusion that you want the audience to reach. This approach to persuasion is nonthreatening, since there is no hint of persuasion. It familiarizes the audience with a set of data and then allows them to reach a state of agreement with you. They do not feel forced to choose between conflicting points of view. In this view, most informative speaking is just exactly that, persuasion by explanation.

2. *Argument.* A second form of persuasion through logic is more commonly associated with the term persuasion: persuasion through argument. This form of persuasion relies on factual materials. In persuasion by argument, the facts are carefully selected and carefully arranged in a logical manner. Inferences are offered as an outgrowth of the facts. This combination of facts plus inferences is commonly referred to as reasoning.

Persuasion through argument requires you to be able to distinguish between fact and opinion. Facts are statements that can be "measured, examined, touched, tested," and checked for reliability. If a statement of fact is consistent with other known facts, and if it comes from a reliable source, then it is generally acceptable in the field of argumentation as a fact. When you reason from facts, you need to be sure that you draw valid inferences from them.

On the other hand, opinion is held to be "clear statements by qualified and recognized experts."[4] This is not to say that expert opinion should not be introduced into persuasion. Quite the contrary. Most classical logicians will accept opinion as proof when the opinion is from a person qualified as an authority in the field under discussion.

Because logical persuasion depends on carefully arranged facts plus inferences drawn from them through reasoning, you might look carefully at the concept of reasoning. Reasoning is classified broadly into inductive and deductive forms. Inductive reasoning draws a general conclusion from a body of specific facts or data. If you want to influence the chamber of commerce to support a day care center for migrant children, you might present a body of specific instances in which migrant children were uncared for and were harmed. You could then conclude that there is a need for such a facility in your city.

Deductive reasoning is reasoning from a general premise forward to a specific instance. The formal syllogism is the prototype of deductive reasoning, although few of us actually ever speak in syllogisms. A syllogism is a train of thought that reasons through some fundamental premise. "All men are mortal; Socrates is a man; thus Socrates is mortal," is a classical syllogism. Most of the time, we shorten the process and in so doing often omit necessary links in the chain of argument. As a result, we may come up with invalid conclusions.

A more modern way of viewing the reasoning process has been advanced by the philosopher, Stephen Toulmin.

> Simply explained, the process consists of three essential parts:
> —A claim, the conclusion you have reached;
> —A set of data, facts and other evidence that would support the claim; and
> —A warrant, the connecting link between the data and the claim.

Because there is no rule for the order in which these essential elements can be presented, it is an easy pattern of analysis for analyzing reasoning. As you plan to persuade or influence through logic, your thought process must be clear to your listeners. If you ask them to make mental leaps and to reach inferences without a clear pattern by which they may do so, they will resist the logic of your position. Man is essentially a rational creature, and he often resists suspicious reasoning, especially if it does not appear logical.

Motivation–Emotion. A second method of persuasion is persuasion through motivation, essentially the appeal to satisfy human needs and desires. Much modern research concludes that this is the most effective method of persuasion. Other research sees it as operational in some instances and not in others.[5] Though there is debate about its relative importance, there is no disagreement about the fact that man is influenced by appeals to his emotions.

1. *Motive Appeals.* Psychologists have attempted for several decades to categorize the basic human motives. Numerous lists exist, and some overlap. There is no conclusion on the "correct" or "complete" list of human motives. We will certainly not add our list to the many that already exist. It might prove helpful, however, to explore some ideas for purposes of comparison and for use in designing your appeals to these motives.

Martin, Robinson, and Tomlinson in their text, *Practical Speech for Modern Business,* list only four basic motives: self preservation, ego, sex, and altruism.[6] Zelko and Dance in a more recent publication, *Business and Professional Speech Communication,* list five: self preservation, economic security, social recognition, aesthetics and pleasant surroundings, and protection of loved ones.[7] To appeal through one of these motives, you must create an awareness of a need to satisfy that motive. Then you must offer the listener a means of doing so.

Monroe's Motivated Sequence, discussed later in this book, (pp. 81–83) is an organizational pattern for persuasive speeches built entirely around the best way to approach the appeal to human motives. Since it is so pertinent to salesmanship, that is where we describe Monroe's method. Even though there have been other approaches to persuasion, Monroe's sequential development is still as effective as any we have encountered.

One important qualifier in the use of persuasion by motivation should be noted here. "Appeals to these human drives are most effective when used in combination. An appeal to one motive is seldom successful in achieving the desired action. The speaker also needs to be careful to use these appeals subtly. As a rule, any suspicion on the part of the listeners that they are being led emotionally for the speaker's own purposes, is likely to defeat that purpose."[8] In fact, this interesting contradiction of human nature probably causes us to reject blatantly maudlin attempts to stir our emotions through sad stories from the lecturn or pulpit, and yet to turn out almost in mass as a nation to watch a movie such as "Love Story."

2. *Suggestion.* An effective technique for persuasion through motivation is suggestion. John Dietrich and Keith Brooks in their text, *Practical Speaking for the Technical Man,* discuss the use of this approach in persuasion.[9] They indicate that in the use of suggestion, positive suggestion is more effective than negative. The personal experience of one of the authors bears this out. In the years prior to her quitting smoking, the most disturbing encounters with the militant anti-smokers were not with those who would confront and argue. They merely called for the traditional defensive response. But what fight could there be against the quietly understated little signs sitting on the edges of desks and counters that simply said, "Thank you for not smoking."?

The use of suggestion in persuasion, particularly in the community, is valuable. Approaches to influencing the behavior of individuals within the organizations may be modified in order to avoid resistance. Dietrich and Brooks list methods for using suggestion in persuasion:

1. Let your manner suggest confidence.
2. Plant suggestions casually.
3. Avoid crystallizing contrary ideas.
4. Suggest ideas that fit the listener's drives.
5. Use positively loaded words.
6. Use symbols.
7. Please and satisfy the listener.[10]

A primary advantage of the judicious use of suggestion in persuasion is to avoid a confrontation with either the audience's preexisting bias or with contrary ideas. You allow the audience to believe that what you want them to do was their idea to begin with. Human nature being what it is, this is sometimes the only way to deal with individuals. It may be, of course, that the suggestion does not bear fruit. In this case, you will have to direct persuasion through logic combined with other means. So, in the arsenal of human communication, do not overlook the importance of suggestion.

Status. In addition to persuasion by logic and persuasion by motivation, we believe that in business especially, there is a third type of persuasion, persuasion by status. This phenomenon appears in many other settings; but the business world, with its presidents chairpersons, is an ideal place to capitalize on it. The fact that someone with status believes something, supports something, or encourages others to support it will often be sufficient to swing opinion.

The notion that status has an important function in persuasion is not a new one. However, we may be the first to speculate that it is equal in impact to logic and motivation. We are not posing this hypothesis from the solid base of a great deal of research, but rather from observation. In the literature, there is a consistent notation of the presence of status in the persuasive process, without an accompanying attempt to classify it as either logical or emotional. It may, indeed, be composed of both of those factors, and hence become an independent classification.

As a speaker, you should be aware of persuasion by status for two reasons. First, in an ethical sense, you need to be aware of the degree of status you may carry into a public speaking situation, and you should be prepared to exercise good judgment in the utilization of it. The president of a large corporation in a city with power over a large payroll, for instance, should resist abusing the persuasive power which status gives in the community. By the same token, if you are involved in a controversy in the community, a good way to begin your analysis of the speaking situation in which you may be involved is to assess the amount of persuasion by status that your opponent may possess.

This concept of persuasion should not be confused with the persuasion your boss can exercise through the implicit or explicit threat to your job or promotion. However, many feel a genuine response to people of stature and influence. A small city recently had a series of town meetings to discuss the topic, "City Objectives for the '80s." The object of the meetings was to tap the citizen's desire concerning goals for the next decade. In meeting after meeting, it was interesting to note the force of the status of the town leaders who had formulated the initial list of objectives. In all but a few rare cases the objective were accepted as written. Discussion was limited, and the general feeling was an unspoken one of "they know best."

With these underlying concepts of persuasion and influence in mind, it is appropriate that we examine some basic guidelines for successful persuasion as reflected in current research.

Guidelines for Successful Persuasion

Because the process of persuasion carries the connotation of manipulating human thought and action, or simplistically "making someone do what he doesn't want to do," it has long fascinated communication researchers and social psychologists. A huge body of research has been generated that allows us to draw some generalizations and to formulate some guidelines for effective persuasion.

Perhaps the largest and most influential set of research came over a twenty-year period from Yale University under the direction of the late Dr. Carl I. Hovland. A recent publication synthesized this research: Zimbardo, Ebbesen, and Maslach's text *Influencing Attitudes and Changing Behavior, Second Edition,* summarized the Yale studies as follows in the areas of the persuader, the message, the audience, and opinion change.[11]

The Persuader. A number of research projects have undertaken to identify characteristics and actions of the successful persuader. To what extent does *ethos,* or source credibility, actually influence efforts to persuade an audience? The following summarizes those conclusions which the research supports:

1. Communicators who have high credibility with the audience will create more opinion change than those who have low credibility.
2. Characteristics that create credibility with an audience are skill, knowledge, judgement on the issue, and trustworthiness.
3. The audience's opinion about the speaker is directly influenced by what they think of the message.

   It seems, then, that if you do have credibility, and you align yourself with a highly unpopular issue, you may sacrifice some of that credibility with a part of your audience. History illustrates this phenomenon in the case of Charles Lindberg and the pacifists before World War I, General Curtiss LeMay's suggestion to use nuclear power in Vietnam, and Jane Fonda's open espousal of North Vietnam's interests during the late 60's. However, the inverse of this also proves to be true. Individuals have gained even national prominence through their association with a particular message or issue. Two current examples are Ralph Nader, who constructed a career out of his initial drive to take General Motors to task over the safety of one of their automobile models. The ensuing issue over his treatment by General Motors created a folk hero, and ultimately the Environmental Protection Agency. Again, during the national grief of Watergate, a relatively unknown representative from Texas, Barbara Jordan, soared to national prominence and earned respect from the mainstream of American society on the basis of an impassioned speech in defense of the U. S. Constitutional process. This link between speaker credibility and message credibility is a very important one, and you need to be carefully aware of it as you speak to the public that your business serves.

4. Characteristics of the communicator that are not related to the topic of the message can influence the audience's acceptance of the issue. A number of research findings identify such things as the speaker's race, sex, age, and status will influence an audience.

The Message. There is no magic formula for presenting persuasive messages. No one can guarantee success. This has not been substantiated by research, (Monroe's Motivated Sequence notwithstanding), but there are some research findings about the variables of arrangement and sequencing of persuasive speeches that can be helpful.

1. Effectiveness is increased if there is initial expression of agreement with some views that are also held by the audience. This substantiates the importance of the audience analysis, which should precede any attempt to communicate, and certainly any attempt to persuade.
2. The more extreme the opinion change that is asked for, the more actual change is likely to occur. Research here deals with how much opinion movement occurs along a continuum from total non-agreement to total agreement. Thus, it should not be assumed that the more extreme measures will necessarily get the most overall support, but rather that the audience will move further along that scale. Departmental managers, labor negotiators, and educators have operated intuitively on this principle for years at budget time. The popular notion is, "Ask for 75% more than you need so that the boss can cut 50% and you are still ahead!" One a more chilling note, Hitler applied this principle to the German nation when he instituted the propaganda rule of "The Big Lie."
3. When the audience is friendly or generally receptive, present only one side of the argument. This same arrangement should be used if your position is the only one that will be presented or if you are aiming for immediate, though temporary, opinion change.
4. On the other hand, if you know that the audience generally disagrees with you, or if it is probable that the other side will

be there to present their position, then you should neutralize that effect by presenting both sides of the argument.

5. Although the research is not conclusive, it is generally held that when opposite views are presented one after another, the one presented last will probably be more effective. This suggests that, in a case where you are on a panel, or one of a group of speakers, as in "Meet the Candidate Night" for the League of Women Voters, you could arrange to be last on the program. (This has been shown to be especially true when the opinion measure is taken immediately at the conclusion of the program.)
6. State exactly what conclusion you want the audience to draw, rather than allowing them to draw their own conclusions. The only exception to this is with audiences with higher than average intelligence. Implicit conclusions are more effective with them. This is probably a product of the resistance to manipulation that more intelligent individuals feel.
7. Forewarning the audience of the persuasive intent of the communication will increase resistance to it. This is an important finding because it means that in formulating the introduction for a persuasive speech, you will need to exercise care in not "tipping your hand" too soon. This does not mean, however, that you should mislead your audience. Your position may be stated, but you should attempt to lead your audience to join you rather than demanding it.
8. Some factors in the message content for persuasive speaking show no consistency at all in the research:
   a. No conclusions about the relative influence of emotional and logical appeals.
   b. No conclusion about the use of fear as a motivator, except when used without a direct recommendation for action to alleviate the fear-producing condition. The reaction from the audience is very negative.

Characteristics of the Audience

1. The intelligence level of an audience determines how effective different appeals will be.
2. Successful persuasion must take into account the reasons that underlie the audience's attitudes as well as the attitudes themselves. In deciding on techniques of persuasion, you

must tailor them to the particular attitudes that you have identified in your audience.

3. People are more easily influenced when their self-esteem is low.
4. Individuals who may be very easily persuaded by you will be equally easily persuaded to change positions by the opposition. Be particularly conscientious about follow-up and personal contacts with those who seem to have given their allegiance too easily.

Duration of Persuasive Change

1. Time will decrease the effects of persuasive communication. Politicans operate on this principle with regard to the intensity of a political campaign. One which peaks immediately before the election is felt to be more successful. The blitz in each state as the primaries come due also serves to illustrate that principle.
2. A complex or subtle message produces a slower decay of attitude change. This highlights what we have already said about persuasion by explanation and suggestion. If an audience is allowed to feel that their change of opinion was the result of their own conclusions, their decision lasts longer.
3. Attitude change is more persistent over time if the receiver actively participates in, rather than passively receives, the communication. Apply this to in-house communication in business. When subordinates are a part of the decision-making process, even though the outcome may not be their first choice, they may more enthusiastically and more permanently adopt that policy.
4. Repeating a communication tends to prolong its influence. This would apply, according to some, both within the content of one communication, and as separate communication experiences. Hence, repetition, restatement, and refocusing are useful and effective development devices to use in a speech to persuade. By the same token, follow-up speeches, reinforcing visuals and memos, and other campaign devices, will help to sustain the influence you established initially in your speech.

Realize that all of these conclusions are based on research studies, and the research is still continuing. Because persuasion deals with man's mind and with human interaction, very little about it can be stated absolutely. However, research findings such as these can give those who wish to be involved in persuasion a reasonable expectation of success.

Preparing the Speech to Persuade

We will use the same seven steps used in the preparation of the speech to inform in our discussion of the steps used in preparation of the speech to persuade. The difference between the two speeches is in particular techniques as you work your way through those steps. The sequence of preparation for persuasion will result in formulating a speech to influence the audience's opinions or actions. Because the steps have been fully explained in the preceding section, we will not repeat them here, but instead will deal in each step with those concepts that apply to the speech to persuade.

Choose and Narrow the Topic. In the case of corporate advocacy, the topic in persuasion is often imposed on the speaker by the existence of a current and demanding issue. If this is the case, then you simply pursue the next portion of this step and narrow the topic to something you can manage, given the time constraints of the speaking occasion.

For example, if you had been a representative of the electric power company that owned and operated the nuclear power plant at Three Mile Island in 1979, your responsibility would have been clear cut. Your purpose would have been to reassure residents and possibly government units of the safety and operation of that nuclear plant following the accident that occured. To attempt to cover that entire issue in the length of most public speeches would have been foolhardy. Possibly narrowed topics for such a speaker might have been to "Explain Causes of the Accident" (persuading through explanation that it would not recur), or "Nuclear Safety Measures Recently Implemented at Three Mile Island." Another approach might have been "The Real Story of the Nuclear Accident" (approaching the audience from the standpoint that the media made a bigger thing of it than was true).

When the persuasive speaker begins to formulate a specific purpose statement, there is greater variety than is available to the informative speaker. The persuasive speaker may choose among several specific purposes: to change opinion, to change attitudes, to change actions. Furthermore, the change may be focused in several different directions:

in favor of something being initiated
in opposition of something being initiated
in favor of something's being stopped
in opposition of something's being stopped
in favor of something's being continued
in opposition of something's being continued
in favor of something's being changed or modified
in opposition of something's being changed or modified.

Your specific purpose statement that you formulate for your speech to persuade should contain both the level of persuasion, and its direction. Examples of specific purpose statements might be:

1. "I want to bring to your attention the increasing problems created by our city's population explosion and to enlist your assistance for my company's attempts to solve this problem."
2. "I want to solicit your participation in our chamber of commerce's project to upgrade the quality of our city parks through expansion of the Parks and Recreation Department's budget."
3. "I am here to ask you to attend the public concert scheduled next Saturday night as a fund raising project for our high school youth center."

Notice that in each of these examples there is a clear statement of both the level of change the speaker wants and the type of change that is being discussed.

Gather Information. Information for the speech to persuade is gathered from the same sources used in any speech preparation (see pp. 30–32). However, as you seek persuasive data, collect not only the materials that will support the conclusion you are advocating, but also materials that are related to opposite points of view.

There are two reasons for this dual data collection. First, in reference to research findings, the best strategy may be for you to present both sides, with a final conclusion in favor of one. To do this, you need full facts about both positions. Your speech will take the shape of a mini-debate in which you construct a series of the main positions on both sides, and then proceed to use the data to refute one side. You will be effective in this approach only if you are fully informed about both sides.

A second reason that you should be fully aware of facts for both sides is more universally applicable. You may wish to use the one-sided approach, discussing only the side you advocate. However, in order to make that presentation as powerful as possible, you need to be fully aware of what the opposition says and their strongest case. It may be possible to turn one or more into points for your own case, which effectively refutes that point for the other side. You may be asked questions by supporters of the other side after your speech, and it reduces your persuasion when you are caught napping in such an event.

Whatever approach you eventually take, it is necessary to be as informed about all points of view as you are about your own. That is not only strategically important, it is ethically necessary, too. Informed advocacy operates from a much sounder foundation than prejudice.

Organize the Speech. The organization of the speech to persuade may be set up along any of a number of organizational patterns. We believe that one of the most effective patterns for use in persuasion is that designed by Monroe and referred to as the Monroe Motivated Sequence (see pp. 81–83). In addition, Bradley suggests that "the motivated sequence, the problem-solution, and the causal patterns"[12] are most appropriate for persuasion. Your choice of a particular organizational pattern may well be based on the types of information you have available and on the decision of whether you should present a one-sided or a two-sided speech of persuasion.

The decision of whether to present one or both sides of the issues can be guided, in part at least, by the current research. According to Bradley, research gives us four conditions under which the one-sided approach to persuasion is more effective:[13]

1. The members of the audience are already favorably disposed toward the communicator's position.
2. The members of the audience are poorly educated.
3. The members of the audience are required to commit themselves publicly after being exposed to a persuasive communication.
4. Comprehension of the speaker's conclusion is important.

Conditions under which two-sided presentations are more effective were reported by Bradley to be:[14]

1. When the audience is well educated.
2. When the audience initially disagrees with the speaker's position.
3. When the audience will be exposed later to counter-persuasion.

Another decision you need to make is related to the order in which you arrange your arguments. There are basically three kinds of organization for sequencing arguments in persuasion. These are explained by Bradley as:

1. Putting the strongest argument first—anticlimax order.
2. Putting the strongest argument last—climax order.
3. Putting the strongest argument in the middle—pyramidal order.[15]

The pyramidal order is the weakest, because your best point is "buried" and tends to get lost. Regarding the other two patterns—anti-climax and climax—the research is divided as to which is the most effective. However, it is important to make a conscious decision about this, primarily so that you will be in a position to judge the audience's reaction and to know which of these arrangements works best for you.

Outline the Speech. Once you have made the decisions affecting organization, you are ready to commit the speech to written outline form. Remember that your outline should be as complete as you can make it so that you can locate the areas needing additional development and research.

Support the Main Points. The traditional forms of support apply in the speech to persuade as they are outlined and explained on pages 39–41. However, there are some additional factors that we mention here because of their particular significance in persuasive speaking.

First, attention is especially vital in persuasion, although it is important in any oral communication situation. James A. Winans, a noted speech authority, stated, "Persuasion is the process of gaining fair, favorable, and undivided attention."[16] William James, the great psychologist, maintained, "What holds attention determines action."[17] The first step in Monroe's Motivated Sequence is the "Attention Step." Attention, we are led to believe, is necessary to persuasion.

Thus, as you select and plan what you will use to support the points of your persuasive speech, you need to devote careful thought to the material's potential to arouse and maintain interest.

Dietrich and Brooks have classified the tools of interest as follows:[18]

1. *Self-interest.* Select those things that directly relate to the interests and concerns of the listener. Appeals to basic human motives as discussed earlier will create self-interest. This is one of the most effective persuasive tools.
2. *The animate.* Using human interest stories, employing forcefulness in delivery, and selecting supporting materials that have vitality. Contrast to explanation.

3. *The familiar.* Human nature feels comfortable with things that are familiar and trusted. Use of comparisons that lead the listener from the familiar to the new are excellent attention devices. A word of caution here, is necessary. People like the familiar, but reject the trite and outworn. Apply familiar data with freshness and originality. A surprise twist to the end of a familiar legend or tale is effective in gaining attention.
4. *The novel.* Although we cling to the familiar, we are intrigued by the new, by the novel. New illustrations, comparisons, examples, and statistics will spark the interest of the audience.
5. *The real and concrete.* Visual aids and demonstrations are important attention devices for public speaking. In years of teaching speech, we have both seen the value of the demonstration, as each succeeding group of student speakers has executed the traditional "demonstration speech" assignment. The speeches, no matter how rough or technically poor, rarely fail to hold interest. There is something spellbinding about watching someone do something as they explain it to an audience. Not all speeches are suitable to the use of either visual aids or demonstration, but when they are appropriate, they should be used.
6. *The uncertain.* Suspense and uncertainty are the human basis for an entire genre of literature and media. Even when we scream in terror in the blackened movie theater, we are delighted with the suspense. Although it would be difficult for the public speaker to duplicate that degree of suspense, skillful recounting of an illustration, posing the rhetorical question, and other devices can be employed. These arouse the suspense of the audience and capture their attention.
7. *The controversial.* Conflict is intriguing to human nature. Example illustrations and examples that reveal disagreement or that call attention to controversy can be useful in claiming the attention of the audience. Conflict is the essence of all drama, from the stage through international diplomacy. Without drama, interest lags.
8. *The humorous.* There are a number of sources of humor, but almost all have incongruity at their root. That is, we are amused by those things which do not seem to fit. Humorous materials that can be utilized in support of ideas in a speech are such things as (1) exaggeration, (2) surprise, (3) superiority, and

(4) escape. In all but the speech to entertain, humor should be used judiciously. You should not substitute ridicule or sarcasm for good-natured fun in a public speech. It should be fresh, interest-arousing, and at times, comic relief in the otherwise serious speech.

These tools of attention should be integrated into the speech, in a natural and unobtrusive way. If the audience notices that you are making a deliberate ploy for their attention, you will likely lose it when the device has been finished. The speaker who says, "Seriously now, I want to talk about . . . " has sacrificed the gains of the humor used. He or she has signaled to the audience that all the material used prior to this moment had no real significance. A good rule in employing any attention device is to lead the audience to the topic of the speech. Hence, humor should have at its basis some real relationship to the subject under discussion.

Fallacies. A second factor to consider carefully, as you select the materials supporting the main ideas of your speech, is the process of reasoning you will utilize in formulating the complete argument drawn from them. The basic patterns of arrangement for arguments were discussed on pages 60–61. These apply to whatever the purpose of your speech might be. However, because the use of logic is basic to persuasion, it is appropriate here to devote some attention to the failure to use valid logic, which we refer to as fallacious reasoning. The persuasive speaker should avoid the use of fallacies in the construction of argument, as should anyone else who wishes to be consistently successful.

The literature of logic and of rhetoric abounds with different classifications of fallacies. These different kinds of fallacies such as "argument against the man," "argument to tradition," "argument by diversion," and others have been discussed and classified in traditional textbooks dating back to the classics of ancient Greece and Rome. It is not our intention to discard all of this scholarship. Rather, we suggest that in the world of modern, pragmatic business speech, the concept of fallacy is more clearly related to the manner in which the speaker establishes the totality of the argument.

We agree with one contemporary author who said, "I believe that in analyzing the objective strength of arguments, a definition of validity will be more useful than the concept of classified fallacies."[19] When we accept this point of view, we are left with the question, "what factors constitute invalid proof?" What would be regarded as a failure to establish a sound claim? Looking back at our earlier discussion of tests for evidence, and at the types of evidence used in establishing claims, we can give some suggestions.

First, regardless of the pattern of organization used in establishing an argument, it is fallacious to reason without sufficient supporting data. A speaker's argument is a persuasive attempt to gain the assent of the audience. To receive validation from your audience in terms of their belief of what you have said, you must present that audience with a sufficient amount of evidence to support your claim. This is true not only when specific instances are offered; but also when the total argument is examined, too. If your claim is presented to the audience and merely restated and asserted, the rational audience will either reject it outright or continue to ask you for more data. An irrational or emotionally charged audience may accept your claim because it fits their emotional bias. But the risk here is great, too, for once the rush of emotional response has passed, your arguments will not stand the test of close examination.

A second fallacy in reasoning occurs when your material is not relevant to the issues you are discussing. A great deal of data, which does not actually relate to the main issue, may sound impressive but does not, in reality, substantiate the claim. Use of analogies and comparisons can be vulnerable to the fallacy of irrelevance. Reasoning that begins with invalid assumptions can only lead to the misapplication of data to issues. The primary question you need to consider in order to avoid this fallacy is, "How does this data relate to the claim I am presenting?" If you are unable to answer that question, discard the data and look for some which does relate.

It is possible to have a great quantity of evidence, all of which is relevant, and still be fallacious in your reasoning. This occurs when you have left out significant or relevant material. This third fallacy is known as *incomplete analysis.* Be particularly alert to this fallacy when you are reasoning from cause to effect. It is possible to omit coexisting variables or alternative causes that would affect the causal relationship, and thus you will have constructed a fallacy. One way to guard against this fallacy is to examine the completed argument and evidence with the question, "What else should I know?" If you identify other things which might make a difference, then seek out the data. It may not exist, in which case, you have not omitted anything. On the other hand, it may exist and throw new light on your conclusions. One very important caution here is if you do not question and seek out these materials, you may have members of your audience who do know them. When this occurs, you have not only been guilty of a fallacy, you have lost your credibility with the audience.

A fourth fallacy is derived from biased or slanted thinking. Be fair in your interpretation of the evidence you present. This may seem self-evident, for it closely relates to simply "telling the truth." However, this fallacy is much more subtle than lying; it is rather the misinterpretation of what has been observed. As law enforcement officers are quick to point out, three different eye witnesses to the same crime may, more often than not, report three different versions of the occurrence. By the same kind of selective perception, it is possible for a conservative and a liberal to examine the same set of statistics on foreign policy and draw two very different interpretations. Be cautious of drawing unfair interpretations and then reasoning from them to fallacious conclusions.

Finally, when you state your data in the structure of your argument, you should be certain to include any appropriate qualification that the data needs. That is, you should make reservations on the claim in relationship to the nature of the evidence you have given. If the evidence indicates a "probability" rather than a "certainty," you need to place the qualifier in the claim. If the evidence shows a "trend" or "tendency" rather than an "absolute existence," or "fully developed state," you should qualify your claim accordingly. (You may feel nervous and frustrated in a traffic jam, but these symptoms, which psychologists would label as neurotic tendencies, do not allow the sweeping conclusion that your personality is unbalanced. A given market fluctuation may indicate a tendency towards a recession or a recovery, but it should not form the basis for sweeping changes in economic policies.) The presence of a qualifier in the conclusion of your argument will not destroy it. In fact, it may make it more persuasive because the audience will be better able to deal with that segment than to try to understand the whole. It is a serious fallacy to draw a stronger conclusion than can be supported by limited data through over-extended reasoning.

In the attempt to persuade an audience, we have already looked carefully at the impact that emotion or motive appeals can have. We also know that it is important to construct believable arguments that will stand the test of questioning and time. It is almost impossible to separate the two factors, but it is important to realize that while they act on one another, they are still two different, independent components in persuasion. You should test not only individual pieces of evidence in creating proof, but you must also look at the total argument and test it for fallacies that grow out of your power of reasoning from the data to the claim.

Tests for Evidence. In the section on speaking to inform, we discussed at length the types of evidence by which you can support the main points of your speech (see pp. 39–41). In any speaking situation it is important that you use only valid evidence and that you draw valid conclusions from that evidence. In persuasive speaking, in which you directly influence others' behavior and attitudes, this is not only desirable, it is ethically mandatory. Since each of the kinds of evidence carries particular tests for validity, we will discuss them individually.

1. *Specific Instance or Example.* The primary use of the specific instance or example is to reinforce a generalization that the speaker has advanced. The first rule for using examples is that there must be a sufficient number of examples. How many examples should you use? There is no magic quantity. As the speaker, you need to ask whether the examples you have cited are enough so as not to be regarded as isolated instances or flukes. In other words, do they constitute a trend or a pattern of human behavior?

An easy way to examine the principle of sufficient examples is to apply it to human relations. Can you validly conclude that all five-year-olds are well behaved because your nephew is? Can you correctly assume that all teachers are mean and insensitive to slow students because your English teacher was? Can you conclude that all engineers are brilliant because your boss is? Most of us would immediately reject these conclusions based on insufficient examples. Thus, the first test of the validity of examples used as support is that there must be a sufficient number to warrant the conclusion.

The second test of examples is to ask whether they are relevant to the point. Each example you cite should directly relate to the specific point being made. If you generalize that the use of helmets in motorcycle riding is a life-saving act, and you cite examples of motorcycle deaths, then you must be sure each of those persons killed were not wearing helmets. If your point is that a particular brand of lubricant extends the life of vehicles, then your examples must be of vehicles using the brand and none other.

2. *Illustration.* An illustration is a narrative, a story, It may be either factual or fictional. The important thing to remember when

using an illustration is that it creates a great deal of interest. It usually has a strong emotional appeal. Audiences usually respond to an illustration. However, in the final analysis, it constitutes only one example of the concept you are talking about. Consequently, you usually reinforce the point by using added evidence such as statistics, or more examples.

An illustration should support the point you are making, and it should be obvious to the audience. If an illustration requires a great deal of explanation by the speaker before the point is clear, it loses its value. The illustration should also be directly geared to your audience. Women may respond better to the story if the main character is a woman. Athletes enjoy stories about other athletes. This does not mean that audiences will not respond to stories about persons from other areas; but the wise speaker will gear his illustrations to the audience he or she is addressing.

Illustrations should be fresh and original. If a speaker begins a story you have heard countless times before, you will lose interest. For this reason, personal experiences and stories are often best because they will not likely have been told by others. However, an illustration from literature is fine as long as you feel that it has real interest value for your audience.

The last consideration you should make in using the illustration involves time. Illustrations, if told well and dramatically, take time. Consequently, you should limit the number of illustrations you use in your speech according to the available time.

3. *Analogy*. There are basically three criteria for the use of analogies, or comparisons in speaking. First, the comparison must be a logical one. Even in the use of figurative analogies, which compare things which are basically unlike, a logical link should exist in the mind of the listener between the two things compared. Second, the comparison must accomplish something meaningful for the audience and clarify the concept. If, for example, you are talking about great sums of money, which is an abstract concept to most listeners, comparing that to the number of days it would require to accumulate that amount at the rate of $1000 a day would create a more concrete idea of the amount. Comparing distances to football fields, or city blocks, helps clarify the image. Third, the use of comparison, like the illustration, should be fresh and original. There are certainly some useful comparisons that have been around for a long time: "the road of life," and "the crossroads of decision," to mention a couple. However, you should avoid trite clichés. To arrest the atten-

tion of the audience, reach for a comparison that is not so well known.

4. *Statistics.* Before using statistics, it might be wise to consider three characteristics of statistics. Dietrich and Brooks maintain that statistics are abstract, dull, and confusing.[20] No speaker aspires to be either abstract, dull, or confusing. The answer is not to omit statistics from your speech, but rather to use them in such a way as to avoid these characteristics.

Statistics can be utilized by comparisons in order to avoid much of the abstractness. As mentioned above, if you use very large numbers, such as trillions, use a comparison to make them comprehensible. Also, statistics can be used along with other forms of support to make them less dull. A set of statistics on what modern young people think about government policies can be dull if they are simply read out as, "27% thought policies on the Olympics were good, 31% objected to the Olympic boycott, . . . etc." But if the statistics are followed by direct quotations from some of the young people surveyed, then the interest value is multiplied. Finally, the confusion that accompanies numbers given orally can be lessened if charts and graphs are displayed making clear relationships between the numbers.

There is a great body of literature on the subject of testing the validity of your statistics. Almost every profession utilizes statistics as a form of proof. This book is not the place to explain statistical theory. However, as a speaker, you need to consider the *source* of the statistics. If the source is reliable, then the audience will accept the information as valid evidence. Note, too, whether the statistic is given in raw form, whether it is presented in interpretation, or with qualifying terminology. If statistical information seems totally inconsistent with what you think to be true, then you should find some collaborating material to reinforce it before accepting it as valid. Finally, determine whether the source has a vested interest in the conclusion the statistics seem to support. For example, on the question of health care, there is a considerable difference in the statistics made available from the American Medical Association and the American Insurance Underwriters Association. No doubt the information is not false, but these organizations are selective in what they release. If you want the whole story, you had better consult a third source.

5. *Testimony.* The tests for selecting testimony hinge on two things. First, by its very nature, testimony must be the direct words

of someone considered an expert in his field. We all know of instances where someone is quoted, but he or she is not an expert in the field. A person acknowledged to be an expert in one field does not necessarily carry any expertise in another. Remember that *competence* is the first component of source credibility.

Second, consider carefully the printed source from which the testimony comes. If you take it from someone else's interpretation of what the individual said, then you are in danger of quoting incorrectly, or at least out of context. One good test for this would be to ask whether the quotation is consistent with the position you know the person usually takes on this issue. If a famous lawyer has always been opposed to capital punishment and you find a quotation in which he sounds as if he has reversed his position, you should investigate a little further before accepting that change as fact.

6. *Visual Aids.* Visual aids are an invaluable source of support. As mentioned above, they are especially helpful in making statistics manageable. They can also supply knowledge graphically.

You may construct your own visual aids for use in speaking. You may also use samples, models, or graphs that already exist as a part of your business. You company might have staff members who can construct such items when requested. However, you may also find yourself in the position of having to make your own. There are several guidelines you should use in selecting or making a visual aid to use in speaking.

First, a visual aid must be large enough for the audience to see clearly and easily. Test it in a room approximately the size of the one in which you will speak. No matter how charming a picture, if all members of the audience cannot see it, it has no value for your speech. Another factor in visual appeal is the use of color to highlight materials on a chart or graph. Lettering and numbers should be in large, dark, bold lines. One should be careful in labeling, too. Make the visual aid as self-explanatory as possible, since labels are usually difficult to read from a distance.

Another factor is simplicity. Visual aids should be functional rather than decorative. The appeal of a visual aid should be achieved through simple clean lines, clear style, and simple content. Remember, the main use of visual aids is for the purpose of clarifying. If it confuses, heightens the complexity of your point, or distracts the audience, it has no value. A good test is how much time it requires you to explain the visual aid in your speech. It should be minimal.

If you find yourself talking a great deal about the visual, it may be too complex.

Finally, any visual aid you use before an audience should be neat. It makes a non-verbal comment about how much value and importance you have attached to your presentation. If it is of inferior quality, your audience will assume that it reflects your lack of ability or your low assessment of them. Either conclusion does little to enhance their acceptance of your ideas.

Plan the Introduction and Conclusion. The same techniques and goals for the introduction and conclusion apply to speeches to persuade as to speeches to inform (see pages 41–45). However, as we saw in the body of research from which we formulated the guidelines for persuasion, there are some special devices which the persuader needs to consider.

First, the research showed that if the speaker reveals too soon the exact intent of the persuasion, he or she may encounter increased resistance. Knowing this does not mean that you should deceive your audience, for obviously, you will eventually have to state your thesis if you are to have any impact on their opinion. It does suggest, however, a technique called the "delayed thesis."

When using the delayed thesis, the speaker formulates an introduction to the speech that is primarily attention-getting. The introduction refers to the subject without an explicit statement of the speaker's intent. The body of the speech develops the main points and arguments leading the audience to the inevitable conclusion already reached by the speaker. Finally, the conclusion should state the thesis.

Let's assume that you have been asked to speak on behalf of your business to a group of secretaries to enlist them to join in the chamber of commerce's city-wide drive for blood donations to the local hospital. You might assume that the group will be reluctant to donate blood. If you begin immediately with a statement urging their participation, they may well reject your thesis from the start. Furthermore, their guard will be up against anything you say in your speech. Use of the delayed thesis could be employed here in the following manner.

1. *Sample introduction.* "Last year forty people died needlessly in County Memorial Hospital. No, not because of inept doctors. Not because of poor facilities. Not because they were neglected by staff. They died because blood in their type was not available in our local blood bank. One of the greatest miracles of modern medi-

cine is our ability to store blood for use later by seriously ill or injured individuals. One of the greatest frustrations of modern medicine is the shortage of willing donors who will share the life-giving substance with others."

2. *Sample main points.*

A. Blood in proper types and quantities can be stored.
B. Blood is often the only treatment required to save a life.
C. Blood donation is safe to the donor.
D. Blood donation is quick and relatively painless.
E. Blood donation is psychologically satisfying.

3. *Sample conclusion.* "Can you picture yourself in the position of saving a life? What about forty lives? You can be the instrument by which another person is granted life. All you have to do is join me in reporting tomorrow afternoon to the Red Cross blood donation clinic, which will be set up in your building. Take a few minutes of your time to give a fellow human being years of productive life!"

Notice that the conclusion finally puts the audience personally into the picture. Hopefully, by this time, your main points and arguments will have created a sympathetic mind set within the audience, and they will be ready to respond positively to the challenge.

Another very important factor in the conclusion of the speech to persuade is the need for an action step. Notice the sample conclusion just given. The audience is not only told what to do, they are given sufficient details to allow them to do the desired action. This must not be omitted in a speech to persuade. Once, a preacher visited an overseas mission. On returning, he gave a highly impassioned speech to his congregation about the need for food, clothes, and other survival supplies for that particularly destitute community served by their church. He became so involved in appealing to the emotions of the audience that he completely forgot to tell them how to go about sending materials to them. This speaker blocked the audience's ability to respond to his persuasion.

A speech teacher who taught both of the authors used to say of basic speech organization, "Tell 'em what you're gonna tell 'em. Tell 'em. Tell 'em what you told 'em." For persuasive speaking, one might add a fourth idea, "Tell 'em what to do."

A last thought about introductions and their relationship to establishing your credibility needs to be noted. When you represent your company in public capacities, you need to be particularly aware of the presence of a master of ceremonies or some other individual who has the responsibility of introducing you to the group. This is the usual procedure in public speeches. When the individual contacts you for information to use in that introduction, be sure you give ample data. Don't be modest. Include any information that will help you gain more stature with the audience. This person, as a second party, can tell the honors and awards you have received, the experiences you have had, and the fame you possess. You cannot very well give the audience this information firsthand. Yet, it may be very important that the audience know these things about you. Take advantage of the opportunity to build your credibility to the audience through another person.

Be aware, too, of how your planned introduction may fit with what this person has had to say. You may or may not want to acknowledge the introduction. It is customary to say "Thank you very much." Some speakers, however, continue to remark about the introduction. Be careful in this. You may end up making the person who introduced you look inept or uninformed if you try for some humor at his or her expense. Our personal preference is a simple expression of gratitude and an immediate attention to the speech which you have come to give.

Practice the Presentation. Just as is true of any other speech, the time you devote to practice is time well spent. Your practice should concentrate on a vital and sincere delivery technique. Interest is sustained and impact is gained through the method of delivery that you develop. Practice helps to polish and perfect it.

Delivery

Merchandisers operate under the assumption that packaging is equally as important as the quality of the product they sell. An old Chinese proberb often repeated is "One picture is worth a thousand words." Marshall McLuhan formulated that watchword of modern communication when he penned, "The medium is the message." So, although the principles of content and organization are vital to your success as a business speaker, you also need to pay close attention to how you deliver the message you have designed.

Communicative Mode

In any communication situation the speaker must show an attitude projecting a desire to communicate. We refer to this intangible but obvious characteristic as the "communicative-mode." It is another manifestation of how oral communication differs from all other forms. An effective communicative mode establishes a bond between the audience, the speaker, and the message. The basic core of that bond is the speaker's desire to communicate.

Notes

[1] David Berlo, *The Process of Communication* (New York: Holt, Rinehart, Winston, 1960), p. 12.

[2] Abne M. Eisenberg. *Understanding Communication in Business and the Professions* (New York: Macmillan Pub. Co., 1978), p. 287.

[3] Robert C. Martin, Karl F. Robinson, and Russell C. Tomlinson, *Practical Speech for Modern Business* (New York: Appleton-Century-Crofts, 1963), p. 70.

[4] Martin, et al., p. 78

[5] Philip G. Zimbardo, Ebbe B. Ebbesen, and Christina Maslach, *Influencing Attitudes and Changing Behavior, Second Edition* (Reading, Mass.: Addison-Wesley Pub. Co., 1977), p. 99.

[6] Martin, et al., p. 78.

[7] Harold P. Zelko and Frank E. X. Dance, *Business and Professional Speech Communication* (New York: Holt, Rinehart and Winston, 1978), p. 275.

[8] Martin, p. 104.

[9] John E. Dietrich and Keith Brooks, *Practical Speaking for the Technical Man* (Englewood Cliffs, N.J.: Prentice-Hall, Inc., 1958), pp. 173–176.

[10] Dietrich and Brooks, pp. 175–176.

[11] Zimbardo, et al., pp. 98–100.

[12] Bert E. Bradley, *Fundamentals of Speech Communication, Second Edition* (Dubuque, Iowa: Wm. C. Brown Co. Pub., 1978), p. 332.

[13] Bradley, pp. 329–330.

[14] Bradley, pp. 330–331.

[15] Bradley, p. 332.

[16] Dietrich and Brooks, p. 172.

[17] Dietrich and Brooks, p. 172.

[18] Dietrich and Brooks, p. 172.

[19] J. Michael Sproule, *Argument: Language and Its Influence* (New York: McGraw-Hill, 1980), pp. 85–86.

[20] Dietrich and Brooks, p. 127.

III Internal Business Speaking

Public Speaking in Business Situations

According to Michael Hanna's survey, company executives generally rate formal public speaking among the least of their problems, considering all the different communication challenges they must meet.[1] Public speaking may not be rated as a problem in some companies because it represents a small proportion of the total communication efforts; or a professional communicator handles the speeches; or (in some instances), the company executive has good public speaking ability. All of these things may be true without reducing the fact that, on those rare occasions when many business people cannot avoid personally communicating, the speech situation creates a very large problem.

This book provides a measure of help for succeeding when a business speech is called for. We shall consider the specific needs for public speaking in the business situations of reports and briefings; and explore the techniques of salesmanship.

In-Company Speaking

It is axiomatic that you must communicate to the public if you want your business to compete in the marketplace. It would be a mistake, however, to overlook the importance of communicating *within* your business. In fact, without effective internal business communication, you will soon find that you will not have much worth communicating about externally. The standard approaches to analyzing and teaching business communication divide their attention between external communication (public relations) and internal communication (organizational communication.)[2] The role of oral communication is important in each and every aspect of a business, including the people involved in the line functions of production-marketing-distribution, as well as those in the support functions of personnel-logistics-planning.

Our main interest in this book is to consider the basics of oral communication, without undue focus on theory and philosophy. A manager must speak to the office staff. A foreman must explain to the crew how to do the production tasks in the plant. A researcher must report to a designer, and together they must come up with the feasibility of producing a new item. Briefings must be given. Salespersons must be able to get orders, and sales managers must be able to stimulate and motivate the sales group. There is no escaping communication's role within a business. People must speak to people both upwards and downwards within the organizational network. This speaking must be done in order to achieve two sets of goals, goals of the individual and goals of the organization.

Individual goals focus on job promotion, job security, job satisfaction, and financial advancement. Organizational goals focus on job productivity, job effectiveness, and organizational profit. The common factor for meeting those goals and for avoiding conflict and downward morale is effective communication within the organization. We will first look at specific kinds of speaking skills by which one can meet individual goals. Then we will examine communication within the organization, which will meet *its* goals.

There is a need for speakers to be able to inform clearly, and to persuade effectively, in order for the business to be able to compete profitably. You can bet your competitors will be trying to do the same.

REPORTS AND BRIEFINGS

There are many situations that call for essential information to be given to someone.[3] In this section, we distinguish between *reports* and *briefings* on the basis of their different functions. A report is information given to a superior as the basis for making a decision. A briefing is given to provide a simple overview or "big picture," without implying that this information will form the basis for immediate action. Sometimes, a briefing may become the foundation for the decision maker to call for future reports.

In a business setting, reports are sometimes called for on a regular basis. A sales manager needs to know the current status of inventories (via sales reports by the company's representatives whom he supervises) before mapping out strategies for each new sales campaign. A production designer needs to have the results of prototype testing reported to him before he can decide how to assign full production tasks to the crew on the line. In situations such as these, the reporting individual is often the only person in a position to provide the information, because he or she has the primary responsibility for developing it.

Briefings, on the other hand, may be more irregular. Reverting to a military analogy, a new incoming commanding officer requires each of his or her staff officers to prevent a briefing or general information. A military briefing is a concise but thorough outline of the status of each branch's operations, possibly including a tour of the grounds and facilities, giving the commander a clear picture of the unit. Briefings are vital to the commander's understanding of the unit, but they must be accomplished in the shortest time possible to enable the commander to take charge and get on with the unit's main mission. After his or her briefings have been completed, he or she has a better idea of what assignments must be given. This, in turn, generates the need for staff officers to begin the process of making regular progress reports regarding the completion of their assignments.

Reports and briefings, therefore, as similar in that each type of speech deals with information; but they differ in the level of information given, the regularity or frequency of presentations, and the information's function or use.

Since briefings are more comprehensive, general, and broader in scope, a topical approach is often followed. The subject of the briefing is analyzed into its component parts, and each component is then explained in turn. Suppose you were the chief train dispatcher and you were asked to brief a new trainmaster on your shop. In your briefing, the trainmaster would want to know how your offices are laid out: the location of the big board upon which the current location of all your train equipment is marked; where the radio telephone banks for communicating with the rolling stock are; and where the shipping control desk is. He or she would want to know your personnel on each shift, and how you handle unusual and unpredicted problems, such as derailments and equipment breakdowns.

During your briefing, the trainmaster would want you to paint the "big picture" without too much detail just yet. For instance, you would probably *not* want to include such facts as these: the receptionist is pregnant and will go on maternity leave in three weeks; the night assistant chief dispatcher is trying to sell insurance during the day and is wearing himself out; the cost of floor sweep has tripled on the latest invoice and the maintenance budget needs an increase to cover it; etc. These problems and situations may or may not eventually come under the jurisdiction of the trainmaster's authority; but if and when they do, there will be time for status reports, progress, reports and decision-making conferences.

Whereas briefings are organized along topical lines (filling in the general outline of the subject matter to complete a comprehensive view), reports are usually action-oriented. Consequently, the organizational pattern of a report consists of the sequence of steps taken in concluding an action, in some ways like the plot of a story. Reports are designed to inform the listener of the progress made towards achieving a goal, or solving a problem, or completing a taks. These are actions and processes, not simply recitals of static and immobile objects.

For instance, suppose after briefing the trainmaster on the personnel assigned to help you run your dispatching operation, he or she asks what your problems are. You answer truthfully that your manpower pool is a good one, but you mention the pregnant receptionist, and the overtired assistant chief dispatcher. As a consequence, the trainmaster asks you to try to take care of these problems. At a later date, he or she calls for you to report what you have done about solving them. At that time, you must report to him or her the story of what you have done—an action—and what has happened as a result. You might report that finding a temporary replacement for the receptionist was a simple matter of calling on the personnel officer. However, for the assistant chief dispatcher, there are tough financial problems that compel him to try to hold down two jobs. It is not solved yet, but it might come down to firing the person and training a new assistant chief. In reports like these, you must follow a different organizing principle for presenting your information than you do for a briefing. This is because you are dealing with an ongoing process and not simply a body of facts.

Reports and briefings are both informative in their basic purpose. They are not designed to persuade or to sell, but rather to convey information upon call. At this time, we would like to highlight a few important pointers for the specific demands of company briefings and reports.

Characteristics of Reports and Briefings

1. *Clarity.* The basic principle for understanding information is clarity. Naturally, a briefing or report is successful in direct proportion to how clear you make the information to the superior. Organization is the key to achieving clarity, and the key to organization is logical thinking.

You should limit your briefing or report to a structure suggested by Aristotle: state your point, then support it. This implies that you do have a point, one central ideal that constitutes that point, and that everything else you say is related to that idea. Let's say you are one of the staff architects in a firm that has the contract for a new shopping mall, and your assignment is the lighting for the shops. In your report, you would be expected to cover the plans you have drawn for electrical circuit paths, the pros and cons of incandescent versus fluorescent fixtures inside shopping areas (not outside in the mall), and the possible problems you firm will confront as a result of the hearings before the zoning board over a proposed new minimum safety standard for wiring conduits. You might have some fascinating ideas about the mechanical and heating plans, or some juicy gossip to relay about a rival's architect's wife, or a number of other things to talk about, but your report must be confined to your assigned subject of shop lighting for the new mall project.

2. *Focus on Major Points.* The Navy has an all-purpose standing order, which is abbreviated KISS: "Keep it Simple, Stupid!" This

slogan means that instructions should be concise, relevant, and orderly. Violations of the KISS rule would be messages and instructions that are verbose, off the main point, complex, or rambling. The way to make sure your reports and briefings fulfill the KISS rule is to focus on the major points.

For instance, suppose your supervisor assigns you the task of making a feasibility report on the possibility of your company's purchasing a computer. You would want to cut through all the possible bits of information about computers and focus on the major issues of whether obtaining one is feasible for your company. Some relevant points you would want to include in your feasibility report are:

> What are the uses of a computer in your company? Payroll processing? Bookkeeping? Inventory control? Information storage and retrieval, shared with sister agencies on the same line? Other?
>
> What are the measurable costs and benefits of using a computer to perform those functions? What are the measurable costs and benefits of your company's present way of doing those jobs?
>
> Can a computer be installed without remodeling space, or rewiring the electrical power system? Would it be necessary to construct a computer facility?
>
> What would the impact be on the company's personnel roster? Would the computer displace any jobs? Would the company be able to reassign affected personnel, or would layoffs result? Would added computer technical support personnel be needed? If so, can present manpower resources in the company be used, or would new personnel need to be hired?
>
> Would company production efficiency in related areas be affected? Positively or negatively?
>
> What are the differences between computer purchase plans and simple leasing arrangements?

These are some of the major points you would focus on. Since a feasibility report is a necessary prerequisite for making a final decision, you would not need to report on the comparative merits of different makes and models of computers; and you would certainly not need to digress about the history of the computer business or other interesting but irrelevant data.

3. *Use Complete Analysis.* An alternative way of stating this guideline for preparing a report or briefing is, *do your homework.* Although your message should be clear and limited to the major points, you must be able to answer questions that go beyond those essentials. Complete analysis of your subject means that you have a thorough grasp of the meaning of the basic facts. Your perspective as a briefing agent or reporter must be broader than the material you have selected for actual presentation. Be aware of the current status of the rest of the field in the area you are assigned to analyze, including the practices and ideas of your company's competitors. Furthermore, you should be aware of the possible implications and interpretations that could apply to your report.

Return to the hypothetical example of the computer feasibility study. Your report could be an important factor in your superior's decision to go ahead with plans to obtain a computer. Therefore, you need to anticipate further questions which may come up. For instance, some questions you could be asked include:

> Do the companies doing business in competition with your company use a computer? How? With what results?
>
> What are the alternative computers available? What brand names? What optional features? What costs, considering both base price and maintenance expenses? What access will you have to service outlets and supplies?

These are a few examples of the kinds of information you could be asked about, not for the purpose of lengthening your report or impressing your audience during the presentation, but for further explanations and answers to potential questions. Use the concept of the lawyer's brief as your model: not every argument in the brief will be made before the judge, but you must be prepared to deal with whatever related issues the judge wants to know.

Your task should be taken with a cooperative attitude, not in terms of trying to impose your conclusions and recommendations on your superior. Rather, you should view your function as assisting in the final decision process by giving sufficient background information and perspective to the specific issues, in order to make your report meaningful to your listeners.

4. *Add Interest Factors.* This advice relates to your style of presentation. In theory, a report is informative, not persuasive. It is designed to provide facts and data necessary for the use of the

decision-makers. It is their job to interpret your report and draw their own conclusions. Since this is true, the greatest challenge you have is to be *interesting.* An unrelieved diet of factual reports has an inherent tendency to become dull, dull, dull! Yet, dullness is counterproductive to your main purpose of informing your audience; because when attention lags, you will fail to get your message through.

Your greatest resource as a speaker is yourself! You can gain and hold attention through your personal style and delivery, IF:

- You speak with authority.
- You speak with force and emphasis.
- You speak with animation, enthusiasm, and variety.
- You speak on a personal plane, using the best oral style.
- You speak with a creative slant.
- You speak with a touch of good humor.

All of these matters are consistent with a factual, accurate, thorough, objective presentation of a report or a briefing.

You can also arouse and maintain audience interest in your material if you present parts of it in visual form. Depending on the nature of the material, any of these techniques and types of visual aids can liven up your performance, from the listener's (and viewer's) standpoint:

graphs and tables	models and charts	slides
chalkboard	demonstrations	film
posters	printed handouts	videotape

5. *Customize Your Report to the Audience.* The principle involved here is appropriate adaptation. Suppose you have to present a report to more than one group. Suppose, further, that you must appear before a small task force or committee of experts for setting company policy, then before a small auditorium of middle managers and departmental supervisors, next before the union hall, and finally before a community service club such as Kiwanis. Each groups wants your information.

Would you not adapt your information to each audience individually? The committee of experts would be a small group of individuals with whom you could meet casually, sitting around a table together. They would be interested in great depth of detail and technical explanations, since they are totally immersed in the subject matter themselves (being experts). The middle managers and supervisors would be a larger group, seated in an auditorium, so a more formally-structured speech would be necessary. A simpler, more general treatment of the information would be needed, since most of the audience would not want the same depth of detail and technical data as the ultimate decision-makers needed. Similarly, the workers meeting in the union hall would call for a public speech, but their interests would be concentrated in widely different areas from those of management. For all these different groups, you would adapt the material to their separate interests in it. The Kiwanis Club membership looks mainly for an elementary exposure to the information, coupled with a high proportion of community relevance and a dash of entertainment. Clearly, each of these audiences would greatly limit the choices you have as a communicator. The size and composition of the audience, the time and space available, etc., must be accounted for in your approach.

Sales Presentations. No matter what your type of business or organization, sales presentations are the payoff. Broadly speaking, even bureaucracies and agencies of the government engage in a form of "sales" in their contacts with the public, and in their hearings before budget authorities. And, of course, commercial enterprises live or die by the flow of their goods and services to the customer.

In terms of successful business communication, sales presentations belong to the category of persuasion. The purpose of persuasion is to influence the audience's attitudes to accept what the speaker wants them to accept. As a general principle, sales presentations are as much in the psychological arena as they are in the logical and informative province. Consequently, the speaker's approach to the audience is more complex, since it is harder to influence a person's attitudes and actions than it is merely to share information from a neutral stance.

Monroe's Motivated Sequence. Perhaps the most widely known and used persuasive speech outline is "Monroe's Motivated Sequence."[4] Of all the possible ways to organize a speech (chronological, topical, problem-solving, etc.), this is the only outline that honors its author by name. This fact is quite an accolade for Professor Alan H. Monroe, since not even Aristotle, Quintilian, or any other person has the distinction of having his name attached to a speaking technique. What is so special about Monroe's Motivated Sequence? Professor Monroe authored a fundamentals of public speaking textbook in 1935 that featured persuasive speaking. His conception of persuasion was so simple to teach, and so highly effective in persuasion methods that hundreds of colleges and universities have adopted his textbook for their required basic speech class. Since then, *Prin-*

ciples and Types of Speech, by Alan H. Monroe has been revised eight times and it is still a leading book on the market. There is no telling how many thousands of college students learned to make public speeches using Monroe's Motivated Sequence over the past couple of decades.

According to Professor Monroe, there is a certain way of organizing your speech, a set sequence in which your points should be presented, which will invariably motivate your audience to accept your conclusions and act on your persuasion efforts. It consists of these five simple steps:

1. Attention
2. Need
3. Satisfaction
4. Visualization
5. Action

These five steps comprise the entire speech outline. The attention step is the introduction to the speech, in which the speaker arouses the attention of the audience and directs it towards the subject of the speech. The need and satisfaction steps are the main points in the body of the speech. They are a simple problem-solution explanation, with the "need" being some problem that needs solving, and the "satisfaction" being the proposed solution that the speaker is advocating. Next, the speech introduces the psychologically motivating element of visualization. Here, the speaker goes beyond the logical explanation of the problem-solution construct and invites the audience to imagine what it would be like after the solution goes into effect. The audience is drawn into personal involvement as much as possible. It is as if the speaker were to say to the audience, "I have shown you the problem, and how bad things are as a result. I have suggested how to solve the problem. Now, envision yourself in a new and different world in which the problem has disappeared. What is needed is a solution to bring about the new and different world that I have asked you to visualize with me."

And finally, and possibly most importantly, Professor Monroe teaches his speakers to *call for action* based on the speech that has been developed up to that point. The reason this is so vital is because it is amazing how many speakers fail to do it! Monroe's Motivated Sequence prepares the audience psychologically to accept the speaker's conclusions, and to act on the speaker's request. However, if the speaker fails to make a request, or fails to state what the audience should do, the speech must fall short of its potential effects. Therefore, the action step, the final step of the sequence, results in a successful finále to the speech. This is where the audience feels impelled to accept the speaker's purpose.

The Sales Sequence. Most of the literature about salesmanship advocates a method of presentation referred to as the "sales sequence," or a similar term.[5] This is like Monroe's Motivated Sequence. Writers usually have a one-to-one conversation in mind between the seller and the prospect. The conversation's objective is the sale of a product. There are many real sales situations that do not meet these limits. Not every sales situation is a door-to-door representative calling on individual prospects, as in the case of insurance, household products, or cosmetics sales. Not every sales situation has a prospect calling on an agent, as is true for real estate or automobile transactions. Also, not every message has an explicit appeal to the prospect to make a purchase at its conclusion. There are indeed many situations that involve groups, not individuals. There are sales campaigns, with permanently ongoing messages to a general public (advertising and public relations), wherein single messages exist for purposes other than a call to an immediate decision to act.

Nevertheless, there is an intuitive wisdom about the idea of a sales sequence. Within the selling situation, in whatever setting, there is a predominantly persuasive intent. The sales sequence itself is the development of a series of communicative meanings leading up to a decision. This corresponds to the principles of persuasion theory, which have been well-documented in scholarly research. Also, there is an internal goal or motive in business, the profit motive, which is based *in toto* upon the sales component of the American business system. Therefore, we will now present the introduction of the sales sequence as an element of internal communication in business.

The sales sequence is a series of steps consisting of six basic elements:

Pre-approach. Market analysis; identification of prospects (potential customers); analysis of prospect's needs and resources; planning a strategy for approaching the prospect, and making the sale.

Opening. Making contact with the prospect. Establishing credibility as a salesperson that should be listened to. Exposing the product to the prospect. ("Product" refers to whatever is being sold, whether an item or a service.)

Demonstration. Informing the prospect about the sales features of the product, its uses and values.

Offer. Proposing a sale or contract with the prospect.

Answer Objections and Questions. Identifying elements of prospect's resistance to the sale, and removing them.

Close the Sale and Follow-up. Striking an acceptable bargain; making the exchange of the product for the consideration agreed on. Providing service after the sale; establishing an ongoing customer relationship; developing future sales sequences with customer.

Let us take a closer look at this sales sequence, component by component, to gain a better understanding of the persuasive process in the successful sales situation.

1. *Pre-Approach.* The salesperson has a product or service to sell, and a territory. Within the territory, there is a population of people, some of whom are prospects and some of whom are not. It makes little sense to waste time trying to sell the product to non-prospects.

The identification of prospects depends on a number of factors, including the nature of the product, its cost, its uses and merits. The prospects and their demographic characteristics, including age, sex, socio-economic class, residence location, and dispersal must be determined. The competition is another important factor. This information is needed to analyze the sales strategy you may use, including the manner of approach, demonstration, offer, answering objections, and closing. Basically, the pre-approach analyzes the best way to match up your product with the prospects who are most likely to need and want it, in preference over the competing products.

The pre-approach step in the sales sequence is analogous to the audience analysis step in persuasion theory, since in the sales situation, the prospect is the audience for your sales message.

2. *Opening.* The opening is analogous to the speech introduction in persuasion theory. There is an added complication that in many sales situations, the salesperson has to introduce himself or herself to the prospect first and then establish a strong enough motivation for the prospect to agree to engage in further talk about the product. Suffice it to say that "cold" selling is a difficult and frustrating

task. It is hard to conceal the ultimate purpose of the contact, and most prospects decline to cooperate in being persuaded to buy. For this reason, "cold" selling is a high turnover job, since few of us have the power to succeed consistently, and most of us lack the ability to tolerate continued frustration and rejection.

But the selling situation is not limited to this aspect of direct sales. There are more stable situations, where the prospect decides to enter the market and shop for a product, or where the nature of the sales situations is more continuous and institutionalized in the structure of the social environment.

Thus, the opening serves to establish the first contact between the seller and the prospect. In this initial contact, the seller must establish credibility as an acceptable source in the eyes of the prospect, and the product must be introduced to the prospect.

Establish credibility. In *The Art of Rhetoric,* Aristotle wrote that the character of the speaker is the most persuasive form of proof. If the speaker possesses *ethos* (the term Aristotle used for the speaker's personal believability), then his words will be accepted by the audience. The classical Greek philosopher went on to explain that a speaker's *ethos* is derived from three components: his knowledge, his honesty, and his goodwill to the audience. If the audience perceives that the speaker knows what he or she is talking about, is telling the truth, and has the audience's best interest at heart, then the message will be completely persuasive.

Unfortunately, sales, as a category of professions, labors under a public perception of low *ethos.* "Would you buy a used car from this man?" was a devastating commentary on Richard Nixon during the height of the Watergate crisis. The insult rested on the mismatch between selling used cars and the office of the Presidency of the United States.

Yet salespersons, as a class of professional people, are not any more or less honest in reality than any other class. The only point we are making is that you must overcome the public perception of a low *ethos* if you wish to make a sale. This task is aided in many ways. You may be associated with a firm or product with a good reputation, and if so, you should keep that connection between yourself and the highly respected firm up front. You may be in a continuous and ongoing sales situation in which you can establish a deeper relationship and reputation with your customers and prospects.

There are some things you can do to make your opening better or worse for yourself and your *ethos.* First impressions do count in the selling situation. Studies show that attire and appearance are silent witnesses to a person's credibility.

Ronald E. Bassett found that individuals wearing "high status" clothing (suits and ties, etc.) were able to get strangers to do simple requests much more readily than they could while wearing "low status" clothing (blue jeans, work shirts, etc.). Bassett concluded that clothing alone makes a big difference in first impressions by providing basic information clues about the wearer's age, sex, status, attitudes, and other important factors.[6] Therefore, you completely control you wardrobe for your sales openings and your first impressions on the prospect.

You can emphasize your goodwill to the prospect. It is no secret that the seller stands to gain by making a sale; but the prospect must not get the impression that your main concern is your own gain and not his or her well-being. Your pre-approach should prevent you from making an opening to a non-prospect, whose interests would not be served by buying your product. Presumably, your identification of prospects should lead you to potential customers who have legitimate needs and desires for your product, who are viable in terms of their resources to enter a bargain, and who can be shown valid reasons to prefer your offer over those of your competitors.

More importantly, you can establish your credibility through demonstrating competence. If you do not know your own product, or your prospect's potential uses and values for it, you will have no grounds for expecting the prospect to deal further with you.

In short, to introduce your own credibility as acceptable, you must overcome a stereotyped presumption against your *ethos* by building an image of trustworthiness, competent knowledge, and sincere goodwill for the prospect. If you fall down on *any one* of these, you can "fold your tent" and leave.

Introduce the Product to the Prospect. At some early point, you must reveal the product you wish to discuss with the prospect. There are very few objects or events with intrinsic interest factors. You must use the opening to link the prospect's needs and desires to your product. You must answer this question: "Why should the prospect be willing to give time to consider this product? What's the connecting link between the prospect and what I am selling?" Unless a personal identification is aroused, the prospect will have no reason to grant you an audience.

3. *Demonstration.* In this stage of the sales sequence, you inform the prospect about the product, its sales features, its uses, and its values. In this step, there must be a blend between a purely factual statement about the product ("This is a widget, at $14.95."), and sales-oriented claims about the product ("This is a the best widget on the market . . . It will improve your sex life and prevent dandruff . . . The competition's widget costs twice as much . . . etc."). Needless to say, the blend between fact and interpretation is the essence of persuasion; but it is also the place where the salesperson must walk a fine line between not being persuasive enough (thus losing the sale), and being too aggressive or being untruthful. This fine line of distinction is itself situational, depending on the factors of the salesperson's credibility, the inherent features of the product, and the attitudes and other traits of the prospect. These may vary from situation to situation; what is too much for one prospect may be insufficient for the next.

There is also an ethical issue involved. The issue is not whether the salesperson's function as a persuader is right. In our systems of law, business, and morality, there is no criticism of legitimate attempts to influence. The salesperson's function is to demonstrate, offer, and sell a product to a prospective customer. It is not the salesperson's obligation to point out the drawbacks of his product to a prospect, or the advantages of the competitor's product. We live in a competitive, advocative society. *Caveat emptor* is a legal principle of "let the buyer beware," which is not an automatic indictment of the business of selling. Instead, the presumption is that the prospect has the right to decide to buy or not to buy, and to be aware of the consequences of the decision.

The ethical issue is in the nature and quality of appeals made during the demonstration to the prospect. It is unethical, and illegal, to misrepresent the product or defraud the prospect. If the buyer has the right to choose, the presumption is that there must be an honest basis given for making the choice. If your demonstration overclaims the product's uses and benefits, and deceives the prospect, you are open to charges of unethical conduct if not criminal conduct.

Connect your Product to the Prospect's Values. In analyzing the proper pitch to make in the demonstration, the salesperson must determine the uses and values of the product for the prospect. On a factual level, it is usually easy enough to show the uses of the product. It is in claiming that the product is of value to the prospect—of great enough value for the prospect to sign a contract and pay cash for it—that persuasion takes place. Values are invariably psychologically established; we are all ego-involved in what we hold valuable and what we hold to be of no value. For instance, an automobile is basic transportation. However, the value of a particular model of automobile for a prospect goes beyond mere transportation. The prospect sees social value in driving a new car instead of an old one; family value in a particular model's safety and comfort options; economic costs and values in the gasoline-mileage ratings and the depreciation factor. Car salespersons have a million stories about cars bought and sold because "the wife liked the color of the upholstery," or similar seemingly-trivial reasons, which were actually the greatest values of concern to the customer.

What are the leading bases for values? What motivates people to act in a selling situation? In the following discussion we shall trace the findings of psychological theory and research to outline the main sources of people's motivations to act—that is, basic values.

1. *Psychological Needs.* According to the famous social psychologist, Abraham Maslow, there are five basic human needs.[7] They are integrated together into a hierarchy, so that when a person fulfills one need, the next higher need dominates action. Each need constitutes a strong drive to action to satisfy that need.

Maslow's hierarchy of five basic human needs is as follows:

> *Physiological.* The first basic need is survival. People are driven to obtain what is needed for physical survival—food, water, shelter. A starving person is motivated to seek food before any other need is met.
>
> *Safety.* Psychologically, safety ranks next. Once survival is obtained, it must be secured. Protection from threat and danger is the next highest need. This includes psychological perceptions of threat as well as actual physical threat. People are driven to protect their personalities from destructive threats as well as placing locks on their doors at night.
>
> *Love.* Once a person is physiologically provided for, and secure, the next strongest motive is the need to love and to be loved. This is the impulse to establish a bond with a mate, and a family.
>
> *Esteem.* The fourth level of need is a certain level of standing or status among peers and the community. A person wants to be respected and appreciated, promoted, rewarded, and recognized as a worthy citizen.

Self-Actualization. Finally a person seeks to reach a state of self, of personhood—to enjoy, to achieve, to create a sense of being above and beyond the humdrum routine existence of life. Self-actualization explains why the farmer likes to play a fiddle at the square dance, or the banker photographs sunsets—while the professional musician plants a garden and an artist collects stamps! For every individual, the mode of self-actualization is totally unique and personalized, but every person is driven to actualize himself or herself in some manner as a strong motive in life.

The meaning of this hierarchy of human needs is obvious in the selling situation. If the sales demonstration can establish that the product fulfills any one of these needs, there will be a high predisposition on the part of the prospect to buy it!

2. *System Values.* Political bodies or corporate units must base decisions to pass laws or purchase goods on certain system values. These values also apply to individuals or other selling situations. The basis of these values is cost-benefit analysis. If your sales sequence deals with a system, you need to consider this factor. A proposed action affecting the policies governing a system should be done, IF:

It achieves an advantage in fulfilling a system goal *faster.*
It achieves an advantage in fulfilling a system goal *more economically.*
It achieves an advantage in fulfilling a system goal *more efficiently.*

Decision-making accepts a positive cost benefit ratio as the legitimate goal of the system. In deliberating over methods of fulfilling goals, the criteria of speed, cost, and efficient operation determine which action should be adopted. For instance, if personnel medical welfare is the goal of the corporation, proposals for company health policies would be compared along those lines. Would Company X's health care plans be better than Company Y's? To make the decision, these and other proposals would be tested by whether they achieve the goals of medical care coverage for the recipients in the shortest time, or at the lowest cost, or with the most efficient operation and administration.

In the selling situation, you should show the prospect that the product fulfills a goal, or a need, faster, cheaper, or better, than the prospect now is able to do; and also faster, cheaper, or better, than the competitive products offered to the prospect. These system values are indeed compelling arguments for human motivation in many selling situations.

4. *Offer.* This is the proposal to sell a product for a certain consideration. An offer is one of the legal requirements of a contract, and it is also the starting point for further bargaining if the prospect rejects the offer. In some selling situations, you have little or no leeway for negotiating or bargaining; in others, there may be many possible options open for negotiation.

If the offer is accepted, then the sale can be closed by exchanging the product for the prospect's consideration—cash, terms, barter, or whatever.

From the standpoint of persuasion and salesmanship, the offer shall always be a free choice for the prospect. If the prospect is not free to make a choice, then the situation is not a selling situation, but something else. The prospect who is offered a product under hypnosis or intoxication is not responsible for upholding the agreement later. A prospect who is coerced to accept an offer by gunpoint, extortion or blackmail, has not *bought* the product; he has been *robbed.* A sale exists when an offer to see is freely accepted by the prospect, and the product and the consideration are exchanged.

5. *Answer Objections and Questions.* Since the previous paragraph has established that the prospect has the choice to accept the offer, it follows that the prospect is also free to decline the offer. When that occurs, as it often does, then the next step is to attempt to learn why there is resistance to the sale, and to overcome the resistance.

Compromise. The usual solution to an objection is to compromise between the seller and the buyer. The buyer could offer to pay a lower price than that stated by the seller. This development is very encouraging, because it signifies that the prospect indeed sees the usefulness and values of the product, as intended by the demonstration. The only issue is how great a value the prospect places on it. In some situations, such as Mexican *mercado,* the selling situation is marked by haggling. Most objects are deliberately priced at double the expected return, or even more; the experience of arriving at a mutually agreeable price through sharp trading is more enjoyable than selling the object outright to a customer at the asking price. In a typical American trading session, the latitude for bargaining is considerably less. Often, real estate, automobile, and other big-ticket consumer items can be discounted 5–10% via the bargaining process. In other situations, such as wholesale marketing, a similar process is employed to a greater or lesser degree to reach a mutually satisfactory transaction. Not every bargaining session ends in a sale, however, since there may be too great a gap between the "bottom line," what the seller will accept and what the prospect is willing to pay.

Sweeten the Pot. When the prospect's resistance to an offer of a product for sale is based on some strongly held value, it is sometimes possible for you to learn what the prospect thinks he or she would lose by the deal. Then, you find a way to satisfy that value, and clear the way for agreement on the original offer. Imagine a family is looking at a house for sale and likes it very much, but stubbornly resists it. The broker determines that the house does not have the proper facilities to accomodate an elderly relative who will soon live with the family. Since the house appears to be adequate otherwise, an effective strategy might be to consult a home builder for an estimate about the feasibility of remodeling the house to suit the special need. Then the bargaining could pivot on the remodeling arrangements, which could then lead to closing the original deal.

6. *Closing and Follow-up.* These are the culmination of a sales sequence. Not every selling situation requires a follow-up, of course; in some, it is part of the offer. Closing a sale should be the occasion for mutual congratulations between the salesperson and the prospect (now a customer), since the salesperson has successfully persuaded the prospect, and the prospect has purchased a product he or she has just been shown to be useful, valuable, for an acceptable consideration.

Notes

[1] Michael S. Hanna, "Speech Communication Training Needs in the Business Community," *Central States Speech Journal,* 29 (Fall, 1978), p. 171.

[2] See Alfred D. Huston and Robert A. Sandberg, *Effective Speaking in Business* (NY: Prentice-Hall, 1955) for a typical treatment.

[3] See Roger P. Wilcox, *Oral Reporting in Business and Industry* (Englewood Cliffs, NY: Prentice-Hall, 1967), for a book-length treatment of the subject.

[4] Douglas Ehninger, Alan H. Monroe, and Bruce E. Gronbeck, *Principles and Types of Speech, Eighth Ed.* (Glenview, IL: Scott, Foresman, 1978).

[5] See Ch. 5, Huston and Sandberg.

[6] Ronald E. Bassett, "Effects of Source Attire on Judgments of Credibility," *Central States Speech Journal,* 30 (Fall, 1979), pp. 282–285.

[7] Abraham H. Maslow, *Motivation and Personality* (NY: Harper, 1954); *Toward a Psychology of Being* (Princeton, NJ: Van Nostrand, 1962).

NTC COMMUNICATION BOOKS

Speech Communication

Contemporary Speech, *HopKins and Whitaker*
Creative Speaking, *Buys, et al.*
Getting Started in Public Speaking, *Prentice and Payne*
Listening by Doing, *Galvin*
Literature Alive!, *Gamble and Gamble*
Person to Person, *Galvin and Book*
Person to Person Workbook, *Galvin and Book*
Self-Awareness, *Ratliffe and Herman*
Speaking by Doing, *Buys, Sills and Beck*

Business Communication

Business Communication Today!, *Thomas and Fryar*
Effective Group Communication, *Ratliffe and Stech*
Handbook for Business Writing, *Baugh, Fryar and Thomas*
Successful Business Speaking, *Fryar and Thomas*
Successful Business Writing, Sitzmann
Successful Interviewing, *Sitzmann and Garcia*
Successful Problem Solving, *Fryar and Thomas*
Working in Groups, *Ratliffe and Stech*

For further information or a current catalog, write:
National Textbook Company
4255 West Touhy Avenue
NTC Lincolnwood, Illinois 60646-1975 U.S.A.